MYSTICISM:
OLD AND NEW

MYSTICISM:
OLD AND NEW

By

ARTHUR W. HOPKINSON

Bene qui latuit bene vixit

KENNIKAT PRESS
Port Washington, N. Y./London

MYSTICISM: OLD AND NEW

First published in 1946
Reissued in 1971 by Kennikat Press
Library of Congress Catalog Card No: 77-118528
ISBN 0-8046-1151-3

Manufactured by Taylor Publishing Company   Dallas, Texas

PREFACE

THIS is not a treatise on Mysticism. It would be presumption on my part to attempt anything so ambitious. It may be doubted, also, whether there is any call for a restatement of the nature of mysticism, or of its essential place in the religious life of mankind. The work of Dr. Inge, Evelyn Underhill, Professor Peers and others has been so thorough that, for the present age, it is not likely to be superseded. The past fifty years have been rich in English writings about Christian mysticism. Whether there is an opening for further treatises, by men of other races, on mysticism of other types is a matter which need not concern us here.

In any case, I would wish to make it plain that I have set myself a much more modest task than to write on mysticism in general, or even on the English flowering of Christian mysticism. The concern of this book is with a certain popular assumption—the assumption that there is something incompatible in the claims of mysticism and of institutionalism ; the religion of experience, and the religion of authority. It is an assumption which is particularly prevalent at the present time, when the boast that " I have no use for institutional religion " is often accepted as a sign of hankering after something higher. But it is an assumption which has failed to prove its validity, and must be questioned.

Those best qualified to find an answer are, undoubtedly, the men and women who have reached the highest standards in spiritual experience, the mystics themselves. Were they —are they—conscious of any incompatibility between their love for the Head and their loyalty to the Body ?

That is the enquiry which this book pursues. It would not be fair to consider only those mystics who were definitely and unmistakeably church-folk. We must also include some whose allegiance to any one branch of the Church was uncertain ; though it will probably appear that they had no desire to abrogate from their religious life the element of Authority. Some of the witnesses summoned are English only in translation : but Thomas à Kempis, Albert Schweitzer and others have been adopted as part of our devotional heritage ; nowhere are they more fully appreciated than in Britain.

My aim is to find an answer to a question, rather than to find arguments to prove a case. But if, in this search for an answer, we are led to jettison the assumption of incompatibility in the aspects of religion under consideration, I feel that we shall have achieved something of real value and practical usefulness for the time of mental and moral turmoil which always follows a time of war.

Part I gives an introductory outline of what is meant by mysticism, comparing it with other avenues of approach to God. In Part II mysticism is seen at work in the lives of some of the greater and lesser mystics. They bear their own witness. In Part III there is an attempt made to apply the conclusions reached in the, preceding Parts ; first, in regard to worship ; secondly, in regard to the mystical interpretation of an institutional book. Mystical meditation is liable to become mere introspective musing unless it has a given object and a given form. On the other hand, even the Bible cannot rest on the letter alone ; it must be read in the same Spirit by whose aid it was written. There is no limit to the mystical understanding of the Scriptures, both of the Old and the New Covenant. The two meditations given in chapters 9 and 10 are, therefore, an integral part of this attempt to show that it is untrue to suggest that mysticism is always unpractical, and that institutionalism is always practical, not to say profit seeking.

In stating a case or writing a treatise it is necessary to give references and add notes. But in a book of simple enquiry I feel justified in applying the principle of " do as you would be done by ", and reducing to a minimum those ·tributes to scholarly convention which for my part I often find so distracting. I have, however, added at the end of this book a short bibliography, and amplified it with explanations. This will, I hope, be accepted not only by conscientious students as a contribution towards meeting their legitimate claims, but also by those living writers herein quoted or used, as an acknowledgment of my debt to them. The references and quotations will be found in the books mentioned in the bibliography, by those readers who are painstaking enough to seek them.

Lastly, I wish to dedicate this book and its writer, in love and gratitude to " The Abbess ".

A. W. H.

Abbot's Quay, Wareham,
Feast of the Transfiguration, 1944.

CONTENTS

THE QUEST

MAN is by nature a questioning animal. We know it, whether we look within or without. Introspection and observation tell the same tale. We are indelibly interrogative. Even the most thoughtless have their moments of misgiving, when they are forced to ask questions of life. *Let us eat and drink ; for to-morrow we die ;* and then, what ? In times of sickness or crisis, especially, it seems impossible to escape the instinct of enquiry which makes men want to know why they are here, how they are meant to live, whither they are destined to go. The stifling of this instinct of enquiry is a crime that we are liable to commit against others : it is the supreme crime of mental and spiritual suicide when we commit it against ourselves. For it is through questioning that progress is made, that life becomes purposeful and comprehensible. In a word, man is only truly man in so far as he asks questions, seeks answers, and pursues *the way of understanding*.

From the moment that our earliest ancestor emerged from the anthropoid-ape stage, and could be called *homo sapiens*, he began to ask questions. The first movement of thought is founded on the craving to know. Naturally, the earliest quest of knowledge was hesitant ; and men found crude and primitive answers to the questions that were puzzling them. The little child's enquiry, " Mummie, where did I come from ? " has re-echoed down the ages. There has never been a time when men have not wanted to discover some explanation of the world in which they live ; or rather, of that fragment of the world which falls within the circuit of their apperception. Why is it dark at one time and light at another ? Why are some seasons hot and others cold ? What causes the storm or the earthquake ?

All these puzzles occupied the earliest thoughts of the earliest thinkers. But the thinkers were all men, no such thoughts troubled the rest of creation. It was in asking questions that man proved himself man.

Baby-intelligence is always self-centred. Everything, from a rattle to the stars is " for baby ". So we find that in the babyhood of humanity the conundrums of life were solved by myths and other devices which were close to the centre of Self, but far from the circumference of Reality. It was inevitable that man's earliest beliefs should be animistic : he peopled the world of nature with beings very much like himself. Earthquakes, he imagined, were caused by the tossings of some sleepy, subterranean giant. Spring was like some woman emerging from the dark cave of winter, where she had been imprisoned by Winter. Gradually, as it seems, these gropings after understanding took a more artistic form. They were embroidered. Perhaps, too, as they grew more artistic they were developed for art's sake and became artificial, parables of nature rather than accepted explanations of natural phenomena ; just as in the life of children Father Christmas loses his clear-cut identity as the children grow older. This undermining of primitive beliefs left a hiatus in the questioning of thinking man, which science was destined to fill. The argument, or the course of question and answer, was switched round ; instead of proceeding from man to nature, it proceeded from nature to man. Cause and effect were related to one another more systematically. A logic and a coherence in life began to be recognised. As mankind grew towards maturity the childish belief that Self is the centre of the universe evaporated.

Slowly—and, at first, unconsciously—there grew up the conception of an underlying reality, which gave meaning and unity to what had previously seemed haphazard and disjointed. It was at this stage of intellectual evolution (though not simultaneously) that the philosophers of Greece, from Socrates onwards, and the prophets of Israel, from Moses onwards, delivered their message ; a message which transformed the course of human thought. It is noteworthy that the " Socratic method " of imparting knowledge was by the way of asking questions. In Greece and Palestine, therefore, not to speak of China and India, there was a forward move, a similar though not a synchronous advance. The incoherent questionings of primitive man became a defined quest. Thinking had become, at its best, the quest of reality. Man had developed into a consciously spiritual being, beginning to look, *not at the things which are seen, but at the things which are not seen: for the things which are seen are temporal ; but the things which are not seen are eternal.*

Once the thought of an ultimate spiritual reality had lodged in men's minds, it could never be evicted. But history shows how multitudinous may be the methods of its expression : it is a long journey from Plotinus to Field-Marshal Smuts. History also shows (though this is widely disputed) how futile and uninspiring are any conceptions of life which deny to reality the highest of all qualities, the quality of personality. A true sense of the oneness and cohesion of the universe led on to various philosophies such as pantheism or monism : it was a great step, but not the final step. Philosophy is not enough. It is to the Jewish race that the world owes something higher—a world-religion postulating belief in a personal God who is one. Monotheism is invincible, but it has proved capable of development. It is the *I am that I am* who alone can reveal the nature of His own being. The Jewish Scriptures are the record of that revelation, and the Christian Scriptures complete it. When the final revelation came, enlightened men recognised both its completeness and its inevitability. Oneness is cold and aloof if it does not contain within itself the capacity for activity and for love.

> Love is a circle that doth restless move
> In the same sweet eternity of love.

The Holy Trinity is the last word in Reality.

This outline of the quest makes no pretence of scientific precision. It is simply a background sketched in a few strokes in order to show that man's search for God is a quality or urge inherent in his very nature ; though the word " god " has been, is, and will be, capable of an infinite variety of interpretation. General statements about the development of the questioning and questing spirit in the individual are as liable to trip up over exceptions as are general statements about a similar development in mankind as a whole. None the less, if treated with caution, they help to explain history, and they may be found useful guides in the testing of spiritual experience. The study of one form of the individual approach to God, in mysticism, can throw light on the whole quest. As this book deals only with Christian religious mysticism, and its relation to other recognised methods of Christian approach to God, we can now leave the general and turn to a consideration of the particular.

From the first, however, it is essential to bear in mind that there can be only one answer to the question, *Can man by searching find out God ?* The answer is, " No ". As S. Augustin says, " The life of the Christian is a perpetual aspiration towards God." But there can be no such aspiration without inspiration. The Holy Spirit breathes into the spirit of man the aspiration to seek God, from whom " all holy desires " do proceed. None the less, the approach to God, which is in its nature and root a response—He calls, we answer—appears to us as a quest. That is our point of view. It is, we feel, legitimate to treat it as a quest so long as its true nature is not forgotten. Leaving, therefore, the ultimate essence of the approach for later consideration, we turn to an attempt to see the matter from the divine stand-point ; that is to say, to trace the development of the questing spirit in man, remembering always that it is implanted by God.

The beginning and the end of a man's life are often marked by a simplicity which leaves mental adventure unhampered and the gift of vision unclouded. But in middle life intricacies of thought and artificiality of behaviour hold sway. For most middle-aged people life is an all-too-complex affair. Beautiful as is the simplicity of childhood, the simplicity of old age is sometimes more beautiful ; for with it is linked understanding. The true wisdom of the aged consists in a conscious and cheerful reduction of life's denominator. It is a wisdom of simplification that can only come to those who accept the outward limitations of old age without resentment, and have learned how few are the *necessities* of life. The less claim a man makes for himself, the happier is his life ; but it usually takes a life-time to learn the lesson. This simplification is not a return to childhood ; but a sublimation of the child-like spirit.

A child does not understand either the thing he desires to have, or the thing he desires to know. He cries for the moon ; he keeps on asking, " Why do the wheels go round ? " An adult does not cry for the moon; but, until he has learned wisdom, he desires a happiness which is unattainable. He lives in a present discontent, because of the imaginary good fortune round the corner. Many men only discover the difference between the attainable and the unattainable in this life, when they near the threshold that separates the one from the other, the finite from the infinite. Our present concern, however, is with the quest for knowledge rather than the quest for happiness. Strictly speaking, it is always the quest inspired by the desire to know rather than by the desire to have that is exercised in asking questions. We want to *know* the answers. It is a far more satisfying quest than the pursuit of happiness, for it feeds upon itself, having internal powers of endurance like a camel. To formulate the questions which lead to knowledge is an exercise in itself full of satisfaction and enjoyment.

Questioning, as we have observed, is the first-born child of thought. If thought, as thought, should be a joy, this joy can best be fulfilled in pursuing the quest of reality in the spirit of child-like simplicity and mature wisdom. To find a guide endowed with these gifts of simplicity of heart and maturity of understanding is great gain.

There is no modern writer better qualified to act as guide in asking and answering questions about the approach to reality, or the thoughtful response to God's call, than Friedrich von Hügel. The debt that other Christian thinkers owe to him is incalculable. The kernel of his teaching is sweet and full of nourishment, even if the husk which envelops it is tough and repellent. It is perhaps because he is difficult to read at first-hand that so many people learn his ideas at second-hand. But whether they know it or not, all modern students of mysticism are influenced by von Hügel. He is, in fact, the inspirer of many writings about the approach to God, especially about the mystical approach. It is as foolish to try to study mysticism without the help of von Hügel as our fathers would have thought it foolish to study geometry without the help of Euclid. In his own domain he is rather like Edmund Spenser in his domain. Spenser has been called " the poets' poet ", because he is thought to have done a greater work in producing poets than in producing poems. He is not, in popular estimation, supremely attractive, but he has supplied the inspiration of true poesy for many of his fellow-poets. Not all of them have read *The Faery Queen* from beginning to end, but many have caught the contagion of poetic romance from it. In like manner, all wise students of mysticism know that they cannot do without von Hügel ; even while they have to admit that they have not understood, or even read, all that he wrote. He supplies the inspiration of their study, and gives them their " terms of reference ". Above all, he sketches out the true scale of religious values. For mystics have a different standard of

values from other men. They weigh life in scales of eternity.
They know that worth lies in striving rather than in any
facile achievement, and that (to use a favourite word of
von Hügel's) it is " costingness " that counts.

His greatest book is called *The Mystical Element in
Religion*. As the title implies, it deals chiefly with one
method of the approach to God. But he must needs
compare and contrast it with at any rate two other methods.
To use his own words, there are " Three Means of Religious
Apprehension " ; the first, institutional and authoritative ;
the second, intellectual and ethical ; the third, mystical and
experimental. These are the *three elements* in religion. At
the present time, institutionalism, the first of these elements,
is at a discount. That is a statement which no observant
person would question. The element of authority in
religion is to a great extent rejected, even by those who
claim that they have a great respect for religion. On the
other hand, mysticism (of a sort) is in the ascendant. Unfortunately, the fashion for mysticism, like all other fashions,
is liable to be marred by extravagance. " Religion is what
it means to me " sums up a great deal of the religious life of
to-day. Men call it the religion of experience ; without
asking—Whose experience ? Whereas it is on the answer to
that question that the value of mysticism largely depends.
" My " experience is a very poor substitute for the experience of the Body of Christ ; *semper, ubique, ab omnibus*. An
ego-centric religion, and a purely introspective experience
of religious truth never fail to proclaim, in their outcome,
their utter inadequacy. Religion requires that men should
look outwards and upwards, as well as inwards. The
record of corporate experience, crystalised into tradition
and expressed through institutionalism, inevitably becomes
accepted as an essential element in religion by all who are
not fanatical individualists, relying solely on *my* interpretation of *my* experience.

Before considering in detail the apparent clash between

institutionalism and mysticism, with which this book is mainly concerned, it will be well to amplify the meaning of von Hügel's " three elements ", and enquire whether it is necessary to consider any other elements or factors in the religious life. However strongly he presses the supremacy of mystical religion, von Hügel, because he is a realist, does not underestimate or decry the other two. He knows that they are parts of a composite whole ; all are essential parts. The three methods of approach to God converge. But each soul, according to its temperament, finds for its own needs one route more direct than the others. Himself a member of the Church of Rome, von Hügel takes institutionalism for granted ; it is the background of all his thought and striving. Intellectualism, the approach which is no approach until it has discovered self-satisfying proof that the road is quite safe, he treats with respect ; though he brings his own great intellect to bear on exposing the timorous inadequacy of it. Mysticism, by his showing, is the crown of the religious life. It is that final consummation of knowledge which comes as the outcome of experiment and experience.

Avoiding, for the moment, matters which border on the controversial, there is one more consideration to bear in mind with regard to the various approaches to God. Nothing is more certain than that the study of all three elements in religion is a necessary prelude to understanding any one of them. They cannot be kept in water-tight compartments. This study can and must be carried on as an investigation of tendencies, characteristics, abstractions. That, however, is not enough. The more important task, and for ordinary folk the more profitable, is to envisage the lives of men and women and children, and notice how in each individual life one or other of the three elements predominates ; and how a balance between them leads to strength—and leads to God. We begin to find out that what we are doing is not so much to give an account, in abstract terms, of three theological exercises, as to note, and try to understand, three kinds of religious temperament. In religion, abstractions are always secondary to the personal equation. Anyone who has had to deal with converts from one Church to another knows, beyond refutation, that most converts are in truth little influenced by abstract argument. Anglicans, for instance, who " go over " to Rome make the plunge because they have met some clever and attractive Roman priest, and because the services of their parish church are so dull. In a forty years' ministry I have never known anyone leave the Church of England from conviction. The motive has almost always been impatience—an impatience, justifiable in itself, but not justifiable in its outcome.

When this question of temperament is taken into account, and personalities rather than abstractions are made the focus of study, it will probably be found necessary to make further sub-divisions, so as to include a more detailed examination of the many varieties of man's approach to God, as well as to use terms in accordance with the changing fashions of religious discussion. The " three elements " need supplementing, even though in principle they do include the whole range of our investigation. New terms have assumed an importance, in much the same way that the by-products of some industries are even better known than the primary production. At the present time, to give two examples, the group approach and the dialectic approach have assumed a position of prominence. In considering the group approach we are not confined to what is known as the Oxford Group, though that revival comes within the category, and is the best-known expression of a wider movement. It is, in fact, a much older movement, adapted by Frank Buchman and his disciples to present conditions. The Buchmanites have no monopoly ; there are other expressions of the same method of approach to God.

One of the simplest of them is described in Georgina Battiscombe's admirable biography of Charlotte M. Yonge :

she says, " Religion is none the less genuine because it lacks any element of mysticism, and a certain type of piety finds its best expression in family prayers round the breakfast table rather than in the ordered ceremonial of a church service or the secret outpourings of the individual soul." [1] All the same, this religion of sharing has its roots both in institutionalism, the family being the institution, and in mysticism, for it is at its best a combined direct approach to God. A united family engaged in united prayer suggests a very beautiful picture of a harmonised worship. It is a picture of the most intimate human relationship joining in the highest human endeavour.

The Oxford Group approximates to this in so far as the group is animated by the true family feeling, and the members share honestly and fairly. In practice, however, experience proves that only too often family prayers are conducted by one member almost at the expense of the others ; the head of the family is inclined to pray *at* his dependants. True unity is baulked if a son's resentment is roused by his father's habit of praying aloud in the family circle that his erring son may be led to a change of heart. It is not so much that he objects to being included in such a prayer as that he fails to see why his father should exclude himself from it. The implied immunity is unfair. Like Ernest Pontifex in *The Way of All Flesh*, he resents being singled out for the Divine disapproval. The same danger is not unknown in some of the practices of Buchmanism, for it is inevitable that the leaders should find a difficulty in sharing quite fairly with the beginners. They have so dramatised their sins by constant " sharing " that they make the sins of their disciples appear poor, puny things—not up to the standard required. Furthermore, their very readiness to exhibit their own sins may lead to a reluctance towards having their sins exposed by other people. The grace of humility is very easily tarnished ; so that even confession may degenerate into boasting.

In pointing out some of the dangers of this group type of religion, no unkind criticism is intended, for it is a genuine type. To point out its dangers may be one way of rendering it homage. But in all consideration of these various methods of approach to God it is always wise to be on the alert against mistaking earnest one-sidedness for completeness. Our faulty nature finds it so much easier to be earnest about some fragment of the truth than about the quest of the whole.

What may be called the dialectic element in religion is modern in its development, and owes its influence to the Barthian School in theology. To the uninitiated observer it appears to be intellectualism spurning intellectualism, or learned men disparaging learning. Such an impression, hurried and incomplete, does injustice to a movement of which the appeal and the power are among the outstanding influences in the spiritual life of this century. It must be left to another occasion to pursue some of its intricacies and find out, if possible, how this element in religion has, as it appears to have, some special applicability to the needs of the present time.

The conflict between science and religion which marked the nineteenth century was essentially a conflict between intellectualism and institutionalism ; one side appealed to authority, the other to reason. To the popular view it took the form of Darwinism versus the Bible. But both parties in the dispute, as we can now see, based their arguments on insecure foundations. Belief in the plenary inspiration of the Scriptures has gone for ever, at any rate in its crude conception of an infallible book dictated word by word to automatic scribes. Men simply do not believe any longer that the 1611 English version of the Holy Bible dropped down complete from Heaven, or that every part of it is of equal value and equal authority. On the other hand, there is a wide-spread awakening to the truth that human reason is no more infallible than are the varied writings which the Church has collected and authorised as the Christian's

Vade Mecum, the Holy Scriptures. Blatant rationalism is in eclipse. The greatest discovery of modern science is the discovery of its own limitations, which is one of the happy triumphs of modern thought.

Now, the arena of conflict has shifted ; " Religion ", as H. C. King points out in his book *Rational Living*, " has to find its way between rationalism and mysticism. It can have no war with reason ; but it must insist that the true reason must take account of all the data—emotional and volitional as well as intellectual—that a man can feel and do and experience more than he can tell. It must deny, therefore, both a narrow intellectualism and an irrational mysticism. To keep the two tendencies in proper balance is one of the pressing problems of a man's personal religious life." [2]

That is, perhaps, how matters stood at the end of the nineteenth century or the beginning of the twentieth. But, once again, the battle of wits seems to be assuming a fresh aspect. Rationalism has learned its lesson. To-day, it is the apparently warring claims of institutionalism and mysticism which are at issue, and, for the moment, institutionalism is getting the worst of it. " I have no use for institutional religion " is the parrot-cry of modern youth, at any rate in its more unthinking representatives. It is a cry which would rightly deserve a full measure of sympathy if it could be transformed from a negative complaint into a positive expression of unsatisfied spiritual hunger. What is needed is not the extinction of one of these elements in religion but the harmonising of the two, whereby the religion of authority becomes the religion of experience, and the religion of experience becomes the religion of authority. That is the justification of my purpose in attempting an eirenicon.

" Harmony can only come through understanding "— what does that mean ? It means that the world should not be like a number of musicians each playing his own instrument for his own satisfaction, and so producing discord, however admirably each may be playing. The drum is not meant to drown the flute, or the cornet to silence the violin. Each fulfils his own part best by an understanding of what all the other constituents of the orchestra have to contribute towards the perfection of the whole work. Most important of all, each must look to the Conductor, who is *above all, and through all, and in all.* No body of men and women have understood this orchestral view of life, or exercised a more harmonising influence in human relationships than the mystics. It is unfair to treat them as if their religion were one-sided—mysticism *et praeterea nihil.* They were, for the most part, many-sided men and women ; some of them highly intellectual, many of them engrained with institutionalism, and most of them people of practical wisdom doing good service in their generation. They lived harmonised lives, which contradict by facts the popular conception of mysticism as a vague and profitless form of religious emotion.

The subject of this book, and the most urgent problem that confronts religious folk at the present time is how to harmonise mysticism and institutionalism, giving to each its due place and proportion in the approach to God. An attempt will be made, in later chapters, to deal with this matter : first, by the affirmative method of exhibiting these two elements of religion as they work together in the lives of saints and heroes ; secondly, by tracing some of the practical ways in which they can be used to meet the particular needs of the present time. For though, at root, the problem is a problem of the spirit, there are, undoubtedly, practical measures which can help to resolve it. The attempt to discover and define them entails criticism of excesses in both mysticism and institutionalism. It condemns us, temporarily, to enter the realm of controversy, so it is better not to tackle it until the underlying principles of these two sides of the religious life have been more fully examined and valued.

Religion lives when it is God-centred, it dies when it is self-centred. An equally true assertion is that it is easier to divert or sidetrack a one-sided approach to God than a many-sided approach, and that the soul animated and directed by von Hügel's " three elements of religion " has a more sure chance of reaching its goal in God than a soul that uses one element to the exclusion of the others. It is on this account that the very attractiveness of mysticism becomes one of its dangers. Some of those who call themselves mystics attribute to " the religion of experience " a supreme place in the spiritual life ; they make it an " absolute ". This is a claim which confuses *climax* with *growth* ; the fragile seedling of holiness has to be planted and tended in the frame before it can be transplanted to bloom in the flower bed.

This claim of supremacy—a monopolist supremacy—for the religion of experience only too often shows itself to be in danger of confusing the subject with the object of experience, failing to recognise that there are two questions to be answered : Experience by whom ? Experience of what ? All experience must be, of course, by self. I alone can have my experience, though it may be intensified by sharing it with others. But the tendency to identify self, the *ego*, with the object of experience—to assert that " religion is what a man does with his solitariness "—is one against which it is essential to be on guard. *My* experience is little more than my feelings, emotions, reactions to devotional stimuli, unless it is consciously related to its object. Religious experience is not, as countless introverts seem to imagine, experience of self, but of God. That is to say, self-centredness is always the most threatening danger to true religion.

These universal truths have their special application to fit varied types of temperament or character. Balance through adjustment must be the aim, and no adjustment is possible without the knowledge that comes by self-examination ; " In which direction am I in danger of becoming unbalanced ? " The soul temperamentally mystical is inclined to confuse God with His works, the Creator with the creation. In a word, mysticism seems to havè an almost inevitable trend towards pantheism. The history of religious thought gives abundant proof of this glamorous pitfall, and of the number of people who, all unknowingly, succumb to it. So much is this the case that every student of mysticism has to be constantly on the alert against the fascinating lure of pantheism masquerading as mysticism. It is necessary for him to class as " suspect " any writer who, in extolling the immanence of God, minimises or ignores His transcendence. This false over-emphasis on one side of the Divine nature lies at the root of many heresies, like " Christian Science ", which are essentially pantheistic. God, they maintain, is everything, therefore everything is God ; Creator and creation are one : I am part of every-thing, therefore I 'am part of God. God's claim, *Without Me, ye can do nothing*, can be met by my assertion, " Without me, Thou canst not be perfect." The temper of mind which is vulnerable to these deceits of false mysticism needs to be reinforced by the strong defences of institutionalism and intellectualism if it is to be *every whit whole*.

Finally, in these general observations introductory to our consideration of the methods of approach to God, and more particularly of the mystical method and its relation to the institutional, one thing must never be forgotten : we have to consider not only the methods but also the nature of the approach. Is it evolved ? Or is it evoked ? Does the urge come from within or from without ? Where lies the initiative ? Is man searching for God—or is God searching for man ? Is the pursuer the hound of earth or the Hound of Heaven ? Here is where so many zealous souls are in danger of going astray. They concentrate on *methods* of approach, always asking How ? and forgetting to ask Why ? As has already been said, there could be no

approach to God, unless God willed it. He is " wholly
other ", in Himself beyond all human sense and human
understanding. All that men can know of God is revealed
by God. The nature of our approach to Him is that it is,
first, last, and all the time, a response. This is a truth
which profoundly affects the whole question of methods.
In the language of the mystics, no man can discover that
God is everything until he has discovered that he himself is
nothing. This is one of the underlying certainties of
mysticism, which the following pages are intended to
elucidate.

CHAPTER II

THE NATURE OF MYSTICISM

IN the foregoing chapter I have made many references to mysticism, without explaining what I mean. It is high time, now, to make an attempt to define our terms. Such an attempt is no easy undertaking. We can say what each of the three elements in religion is *not* much more simply than we can say what it is. To a great extent we are forced to use illustrations and similes in the hope of conveying a correct impression of something which is, in its reality, undefinable. We might, for example, compare religious life to a railway journey ; the mystical spirit is the motive power, institutionalism supplies the rails upon which the train advances, intellectualism resembles the engine which prevents a waste of the motive power and helps to keep the train moving on the lines. From the carriage window we get an occasional glimpse of the far-away city to which we are travelling ; but that does not mean that we have reached our destination.

How feeble is this picture, how inadequate, how misleading ! Yet it is only by means such as this that we can get nearer to a conception of what these various methods of approach to God are in themselves, and in their relationships to one another.

No satisfactory definition of mysticism has ever been found. Those who know most about it recognise that it has an elusive quality which defies the precision of language necessary to a good definition. A wide definition is too nebulous, a concise definition is too limiting. But Arthur Chandler hit on an enlightening title when he called it " First-hand Religion ". That describes one aspect at any

rate of mysticism ; there is nothing second-hand about it.
The mystic's approach to God is a direct approach, not
dependent on other people or on external circumstances,
but a matter between the soul and God alone. It is this
solitariness which constitutes both its attraction and its
danger. There is the attraction of experiencing a concentration of intention, the all-for-all outpouring of the soul,
unqualified by outward helps, and unhampered by the
hindrances that are inherent in second-hand religion. On
the other side, there is the danger of spiritual vertigo, the
inhuman independence which forgets that the religion of
the Fatherhood of God is self-contradictory unless it blossoms
in the Brotherhood of Man. *We are members one of another*,
and can only be saved as members of a family. The King
can only be served acceptably by members of His Kingdom
in union one with another.

There is nothing second-rate about second-hand religion.
Millions of men have begun to learn their religion second-
hand from their mothers, and have sense enough not to
despise it on that account. The faith by which Christians
live is second-hand. It is a tradition ; that is to say,
something *handed on*, something with the authority of continuity. If we all started from the beginning, and not from
where others have left off, no permanent progress would
ever be made, and the final result would be sheer anarchy.
The man who denies religious instruction to his children on
the ground that they must not be prejudiced in favour of
any form of belief until they are old enough to weigh up
the merits of all beliefs is living in a world that never has
existed and never will exist. The simple, stabbing truth is
that religion without religious education is a chimera and a
mockery : *Other men laboured, and ye are entered into their
labours.* Order, continuity, tradition, and discipline come
to us, as it were, second-hand. Without them there could
be no genuine first-hand religion, for no religion has been
or could be parthenogenous.

Religion is not, in this respect, in a category by itself. There is nothing unique in its recognition of tradition as binding, or of training as necessary. The same principle holds good throughout life. It is an essential characteristic of human nature. The living owe their lives, all that they are and all that they have, to the dead. (The present derives from the past, and the past lives again in the present.) So whether the matter is considered from a secular or a religious point of view, it is true to repeat that the man who declares that his children shall be taught no religion until they are old enough to judge religion for themselves is a fool, for he is not only defying the revealed method of God's working, he is also acting in contradiction to common sense, by trying to reverse the universal law of the interdependence of man upon man all down the ages. We owe life of body mind and spirit to our forefathers ; it is second-hand. (Tradition is a law of being.)

None the less, tradition can seldom give that sense of utter certainty that experience can give. A child may accept what his elders tell him about the buoyancy of his body in water, but his trust will lack the happiness of absolute certainty until he has learned to swim, and proved by his own experience what he had accepted on the authority of others. Experience does not make the fact more true, but it does bring home the truth to the individual. Religious experience vitalises religious truth. What is wrong with the religion of most people is not that it is second-hand, for it could not be otherwise, but that it is not also first-hand. It lacks the supreme quality of certainty. Unless a Christian can say, with S. Paul, *I know whom I have believed*, he can never enjoy the confident happiness of his religion, nor can he ever expect to be a profitable servant in the Kingdom. (He who hesitates is lost ; *the double-minded man is unstable in all his ways :* but certainty spells salvation, and certainty radiates power.) Cowardice is the child of uncertainty, and courage the child of certainty. Small wonder, then, that so many of the mystics have been heroes or heroines.

This all goes to prove that tradition must be reinforced by experience : *O taste and see how gracious the Lord is !* Moreover, it must be borne in mind that both have a common origin. It is a mistake to suppose that tradition is received, and experience is acquired ; that we get one from other people, and evolve the other from ourselves. Both come from the All-giver. Institutional religion, at its best, declares that Christian tradition comes from God. Mystical religion, at its best, declares that experience comes from God. First-hand religion and second-hand religion do not clash, rather, one is impossible without the other. The world needs both the socialist and the individualist ; so does the Church. Institutional religion, without the mystical sense of individual approach to God, is doomed to become formal, perfunctory, and unreal. The history of the Christian Church in the past 1900 years, as well as the history of other cults and religions, is full of tragedies due to this one-sidedness. Not less tragic is the story of zealous men and women, potential saints, who have lost their souls through excessive individualism. They have gradually come to deride God's good gift of discipline, and imagined themselves to be above law. This has led on to a contempt for those of their fellow-Christians whose religious outlook is different from their own, and to a pride which is rightly called Satanic.

If an author were commissioned to write a book on soldiering, he might set about it in one of two ways : (1) He might begin with a definition of the word, and then go on to tell of the characteristics of soldiering, its place and function in the body politic, and its probable developments. This way of dealing with the subject would asuredly result in a very dull book that nobody would want to read. (2) He might describe soldiers ; their appearance, their weapons and clothing, their duties, their achievements, and their foibles. He might recount deeds of soldierly courage, or sketch the biographies of famous fighters. A book written on these lines would probably be interesting, even if it were incomplete and unscientific. Very few people prefer a diagram to a news-reel ; they find soldiering, as an abstract subject for a treatise, dull, but they find soldiers very interesting fellow-men.

It is unlikely that a student will learn much about his subject, be it soldiering or mysticism or anything else, unless he is interested in it. Once interest is aroused, the student will become to a great extent his own teacher. With all the happy instinct of the chase, he will *pursue* his subject. These musings about method lead to the conclusion that the most interesting and profitable way of writing about mysticism is to write about mystics. This is what I set myself to do in some of the later chapters ; portraying mysticism in the working, with something of its fascinating variety of expression through personalities, and including a good deal of what can only be called " semi-mysticism ".

Meanwhile, it is not, I hope, without interest to consider something about mystics in general ; about what constitutes a mystic, and how mystics differ from non-mystics. Here again, as with regard to the definitions of mysticism, the experts speak with many voices, delivering verdicts which at first sight seem difficult to reconcile with one another. Evelyn Underhill, for example, would probably deny the title of mystic to many whom Arthur Chandler would accept ; W. R. Inge would raise his eyebrows at some of the names that Percy Osmond includes in his volume on *The Mystical Poets of the English Church*. Let it be granted that there is a strict, technical sense in which it is sometimes advisable to use the word, in order to correct the misapprehension of those people who are ready to salute as " mystic " anyone who evinces a certain dreaminess in his devotion. Yet, on the other hand, it is not right to shut out from the brotherhood of mystics all those who have failed to find conscious expression of their spiritual experience in terms recognisable as " mystical ".

In considering the relationship between the mystical and the institutional elements in religion, it is not necessary to define mysticism in the stricter way favoured by some writers ; or rather, a distinction may be made between mysticism and " the mystical element ". But it is necessary to bear in mind that there is the stricter interpretation, and it is not wrong. Aldous Huxley is one of the most thorough-going of the writers who would make mysticism a religion *sui generis*. He draws a distinction between the utterly theo-centric mysticism of what he calls " the Dionysian tradition " and the Jesus-mysticism which was the normal type of devotion among the spiritual leaders of the Catholic Church in the seventeenth century. He is inclined to deny that such an approach to God is genuine mysticism, and quotes with approval, " God is to be worshipped without regard to one's spiritual profit. He is to be worshipped for his own sake, in an act of adoration and awe. He is to be worshipped as He is in Himself, the sovereign and infinite being. To worship this sovereign and infinite being ade-quately, a man would have himself to be infinite and possess the highest reality. In practice, God has only once been worshipped as he should be worshipped, and that was by Christ, who being God as well as man, was alone capable of giving the infinite adoration due to an infinite and eternal reality." This contention he sums up by declaring that " in genuine mysticism the theo-centric hypothesis is axiomatic ". The implication that pure mysticism is essentially un-Catholic does not daunt him. Nor would he be moved by the Christian mystic's reliance on the Lord's saying that *no man cometh to the Father but by me :* for Huxley, the One Mediator is a supernumerary. His whole attitude is most clearly defined in his criticism of Bérulle, a great Christian mystic of the period about which he is writing :—

" Bérulle possessed undoubtedly a great aptitude for the mystical life ; but before being a mystic, he was a Catholic. For him, theology, the gospel story and ecclesiastical tradition were fundamental data, antecedent to personal experience, which was something to be bent and moulded into conformity with them. The contemplatives of the Dionysian tradition, on the other hand, had adapted dogma to their own experience, with the result that, in so far as they were advanced mystics, they had ceased to be specifically Catholic. To a non-Christian, this seems the supremely important, the eminently encouraging fact about mysticism—that it provides the basis for a religion free from unacceptable dogmas, which themselves are contingent on ill-established and arbitrarily interpreted historical facts. To certain pious Christians, on the other hand, mysticism is suspect precisely because of its undogmatic and unhistorical character. Bérulle knew and respected the mystics of the Dionysian tradition, but he preferred not to follow them. Instead, he devoted all the energies of a powerful intellect to the creation of a new, mystico-Catholic philosophy of life. In this philosophy, the raw materials of Catholic dogmas and popular Catholic devotion were worked up into a finished product of high spirituality by means of techniques borrowed from the Dionysian contemplatives. The result was in the highest degree remarkable ; but it was not mysticism." [3]

In this attitude Huxley is entirely consistent : accept his premises, and his conclusions follow. It is not our concern to question his premises or to examine his attitude except for the purpose of noting, what his criticism of Bérulle so convincingly reveals, that without the institutional element there can be no specifically Christian mysticism—the gospel story and ecclesiastical tradition are *fundamental data*, antecedent to personal experience. Aldous Huxley's contempt for authority in religion may possibly account for the fact that, though his insight into the technique of mysticism is unsurpassed among modern writers, he shows no inclination to pursue the mystic way.

It is impossible to leave this aspect of our subject without some reference to the word "metaphysical", which keeps cropping up in writings about mysticism. Some writers, in fact, appear to make metaphysical synonomous with mystical. Helen White, the American authoress, has published a delightful and illuminating book to which she gives the title *The Metaphysical Poets*, but in the body of the book she writes about them almost entirely as mystical. Many students of William James, also an American, would feel justified in asserting that he, too, shows little sign of making a distinction between the two terms. The same might be said about a number of articles on this subject in American magazines. But an ordinary dictionary definition of metaphysics is that it is "the science which investigates the first principles of nature and thought : ontology or the science of being " ; and of the adjective "metaphysical " the definition is "abstract". The same dictionary defines mysticism as "a tendency of religious feeling marked by an effort to attain to direct and immediate communion with God ". It can scarcely be maintained, therefore, that metaphysics and mysticism are the same, nor should it ever be implied. So it is necessary to issue a warning against an assumption which appears in a number of American writers —and they, writers of the highest rank. English readers do well to remember that while mysticism has a deep affinity with metaphysics, it is misleading to use the words as if they were interchangeable. This criticism applies only to modern writers, for in the seventeenth century "metaphysical " was used in an accommodated or non-natural sense, and was generally so understood.

After this necessary digression, we can return to the general question of where to draw the line between a mystic and a non-mystic. It is a question which, in the main, I am content to evade. For the moment, there is no need to draw such a line. My working hypothesis will be that *every man is a potential mystic.* It would be sad if it were not so ; for a religion which is to be worthy of the name of religion must include the mystical as well as the intellectual, ethical, institutional, metaphysical, and logical elements, and many others, and man is made for religion as truly as religion is made for man. How this potentiality for mysticism is, and can be, developed will appear as we go on to consider the different degrees of mysticism and the various types of mystics.

Of those who are acknowledged to be mystics it may be said that the greater mystics are men and women who have experienced God, and the lesser mystics are men and women who believe that it is possible to experience God. This is a challenging statement. It is meant to be. It challenges us to think what is meant by experiencing God ; for experiencing God is a far different matter from having experience of God's ways and of His doings, just as knowing God is quite different from knowing about God. The challenge is also a reminder that while all Christians hope, somehow, to experience God after death, it is only the mystics who believe that it is possible, *in this life*, to attain to that experience. Their hope is, in spite of the shackles of time, and space, and human imperfection, to make contact with ultimate reality. That some have done so is difficult to doubt. The witness of the greater mystics is unanimous, though the way in which they try to describe their experience is never quite the same. For each is trying to describe something that he knows to be far beyond description. How they have tried to do it will be discussed in a later chapter ; we must not anticipate the end before we have tackled the beginning.

What constitutes the beginning of mystical experience ? Certainly no one emotion, or impulse, or event : *the wind bloweth where it listeth, and thou hearest the sound thereof, but canst not tell whence it cometh, and whither it goeth : so is everyone*

that is born of the Spirit. Some begin the adventure through
a feeling of harmony with the throbbing pulse of Nature ;
some are aroused by an emotional appeal to their better self ;
others get a sudden enlightenment of the understanding.
One of the commonest ways of entering upon mystical
experience is through a sense of *presence*, a conviction that
there is something (or Someone) with us to guide, protect,
or comfort. Times of emergency become times of illumination. There come to us knowledge and power when we
most need them. The first lesson of mysticism is to refuse
to distrust this sense of presence, for it is one of the great
realities of the spiritual life, a trustworthy beginning of the
supreme adventure. If at first the presence causes fear,
that need not lead to panic, for we are admonished that
fear is the beginning of wisdom. This mystical fear will
lead to mystical wisdom, to the joy of the illuminative stage,
and the rapture of the unitive stage in the mystical way.

That this sense of presence is a frequent experience, even
among the uninitiated, can be proved by anyone who has
the gift of winning the confidence of his fellow travellers in
the road of life. It is well, however, to confirm this statement by two or three notable illustrations of experiences
which many readers will recognise as similar to some
happenings in their own lives :

(1) Sir Ernest Shackleton's latest expedition to the
Antarctic was dogged by many misfortunes, one trouble
followed upon another ; and the climax of them seemed to be
reached when his ship, the *Endurance*, was crushed to pieces
in the ice, and the members of the expedition were left, with
their sledges and three small boats, eleven hundred miles
from the nearest inhabited land. It was a grim prospect
that they had to face, this seemingly impossible journey.
The first three hundred miles were mainly tramped over
the ice. Then Shackleton and five companions set out on
a voyage of eight hundred miles over the stormy Antarctic
Ocean in a small open boat. It would be impossible to

describe the full hardship of that voyage.   The six voyagers
reached South Georgia in a state of collapse, half-starved,
almost mad with thirst, frost-bitten, and covered with
sores.   And still they had not reached the human habita-
tions, which were at the other side of South Georgia.   No
man had ever penetrated a mile inland from that desolate
coast.   The whalers who occasionally visited it looked upon
the interior as utterly inaccessible.   The mountains rose
precipitously to a height of 5,000 feet, and were intersected
by great glaciers and ice-fields.   Yet Shackleton and two
of his companions, Worsley and Crean, accomplished the
journey across to the other side.   It was a feat not only of
endurance but of inspiration, as Shackleton bore witness, in
writing of it later :

> " When I look back on those days, I have no doubt
> that Providence guided us, not only across those snow-
> fields but also across the storm-white sea that separated
> Elephant Island from our landing-place in South Georgia.
> I know that through that long and aching march of
> thirty-six days over the unnamed mountains and glaciers
> of South Georgia it seemed to me often that we were four
> not three.   I said nothing to my companions on the point,
> but afterwards Worsley said to me, *Boss, I had a curious
> feeling on the march that there was another person with us.*
> Crean confessed to the same idea.   One feels the dearth
> of human words and the roughness of mortal speech in
> trying to describe things intangible, but a record of our
> journeys would be incomplete without a reference to a
> subject very near to our hearts." [4]

(2) Captain Johnston and Captain Yearsley, in their
book, *Four Hundred and Fifty Miles to Freedom,* narrate the
hardships and adventures of eight British officers who
escaped, during the last war, from a Turkish prison in the
interior of Asia Minor.   They were a representative lot,
comprising two men from the Indian Army, one from the
Royal West Kents, one from the Hampshires, one from the

Garrison Artillery, one from the Royal Engineers, one from the Duke of Cornwall's Light Infantry, and one from the Royal Navy. The Army men gladly admit that the Navy took the lead. The story of their adventure is told in simple and almost common-place language ; but in spite of· the modesty of the writers (or because of that modesty) it shines out convincingly as a story of magnificent endurance and courage. The account of their hairbreadth escapes and the wonder of their final success makes thrilling reading. It is the postscript which bears witness to an experience similar to that of Sir Ernest Shackleton :

" There is one note which we feel we must add before laying down our pens. Many of our readers will have already realised that there was something more than mere luck in our escape. . . . To be at large for thirty-six days before escaping from the country, to have been so frequently seen, certainly sometimes to have aroused suspicion, and yet to have evaded recapture, might perhaps be attributed to Turkish lack of organisation. Our escape from armed villagers ; our discovery of wells in the desert, of corn in an abandoned farm-house ; and finally, the timely reappearance of the motor-tug with all essential supplies for a sea voyage (when we reached the coast)—any one of these facts taken alone, might possibly be called luck or a happy coincidence ; taken in conjunction with one another however, they compel the admission that the escape of our party was due to a higher Power. . . . We feel that it was Divine intervention, which brought us through. Throughout the preparations for escape every important step had been made a matter of prayer ; and when the final scheme was settled friends in England were asked, by means of a code message, to intercede for its success. We had also friends in Turkey (among our fellow-prisoners) who were interceding for us ; and on the trek it was more than once felt that someone at home or in Turkey was remembering us at the time. To us the hand of Providence was manifest in our escape. And we see in it an answer to prayer. Our way, of course, might have been made smoother, but perhaps in that case we should not have learned the same lessons of dependence upon God. As it was, it was made manifest to us that, in these materialistic days, to those who have faith, *the Lord's hand is not shortened that it cannot save.*" [5]

(3) A more recent testimony to the experience of spiritual companionship in time of need is given by Bishop Heaslett of Tokyo, who was imprisoned when the present war with Japan broke out. At the worst moment of his examination by the brutal Japanese police, when exhausted and at the point of break-down, there came to him a sudden relief : he felt beside him a light and a presence, and received a message, *My grace is sufficient for thee, and my strength is made perfect in thy weakness.* In his own words of witness :

"There was power given to endure, just that. That was the unexpected, promised Presence, the answer to my prayers, the mitigation of my fears."

The sense of a presence is only one of many ways in which progress in the path of mysticism may begin. In the cases cited it was a comfort and an illumination, which helped to save the situation for men in dire distress. Man's extremity was God's opportunity. It must not be assumed, however, that all are as ready to benefit by the sense of a presence, or to welcome an unseen companion as were these heroes whose record of their experiences I have just quoted.

To most men, the beginning of mystical experience, and the realisation of a something outside themselves greater than themselves, is terrifying. They are, as Christian theology would express it, " convicted of sin ". And not only is the sense of a presence often terrifying at the beginning ; each fresh illumination of what that presence means may be an inspiration of fear. Peter had been present with Jesus for many months, called himself His disciple, and shared His work, yet when Jesus' power was manifested in the miraculous draught of fishes, the fuller illumination that came to Peter filled him with a frightened consciousness of unworthiness, and wrung from him the cry, *Depart from me ; for I am a sinful man, O Lord.* A less excellent fear is seen at work in the conscience of the ordinary worldling, who hates nothing so much as solitude. Every moment of his life must be filled with companionship, bolstered up with society ; if he is left by himself his existence is unbearable. In the absence of acquaintances the grip of solitude must be at least relaxed by switching on the wireless. For when he is alone and in silence, there comes into his consciousness a feeling that he is not alone. Reality impinges on the unreality of his life, and frightens him.

The nature of mysticism is that it always implies a return to reality ; it is the solvent of all that is artificial in the religious life. By mysticism the self-centredness of false religion is disintegrated. That does not mean that it dissolves or disintegrates all forms and traditions. It is only the enemy of formalism and conventionality in so far as they are false. It is characterised by no spirit of monopoly, but accepts all that is true in the other elements of religion. It does not offer an *alternative* system. There is no technique of Christian Mysticism, nor is there anything esoteric about it. It is not like Yoga, that " system of philosophic meditation and asceticism designed to effect the reunion of the devotee's soul with the universal spirit ". Its key-note is not effort but receptivity ; not pride but humility. Though men may win for themselves a great reputation for holiness by a self-imposed asceticism, they do not by their own effort earn the right to be called mystics : *Many are in high place, and of renown : but mysteries are revealed to the meek.* The mysteries of mysticism are not discovered but revealed.

It is a misunderstanding of mysticism to identify it with asceticism, or a discipline which has as its aim the acquisition of esoteric knowledge of spiritual states. Another way in which the nature of mysticism is misunderstood is in identifying it, partially at any rate, with some organisation of religious life, like monasticism. To the minds of many people the thought of mystics at once suggests monks and nuns, whereas nothing is more false than to imagine that mysticism is confined to the cloister. Indeed, the limitations of monasticism have proved, in some cases, a hindrance to the mystical spirit. It is not a mere paradox to say that Thomas à Kempis would have been more of a mystic if he had been less of a monk ; in other words, his mysticism was a sheltered and a predominantly ascetic mysticism.

To sum up, mysticism is not so much a mode of life as a code of values. It finds its treasure where its heart is—in God. Whatever may be a man's outward position and circumstances, in so far as he is a mystic he holds within himself a standard of values which is not the world's standard. And by this invisible but clearly sensed possession mystics, in their wayfaring through the world, recognise one another :

> Happy are they, they that love God,
> Whose hearts have Christ confest,
> Who by his Cross have found their life,
> And 'neath his yoke their rest.
>
> .   .   .   .
>
> Then shall they know, they that love him,
> How all their pain is good ;
> And death itself cannot unbind
> Their happy brotherhood.

This brotherhood of love is a brotherhood of adventure. In that respect it fulfils one of the most splendid aspirations of the human heart ; and never was such a chance of fulfilment needed more than at the present time. Adventurous souls are glum at the thought that romance is departing from the world. War may provide one sort of adventure. The danger is lest, failing romance, the soldier's spirit of adventure should become the spirit of discontent and licence after the war. What is to take the place of the airman's thrill ? For it seems as if there is nothing left for the explorer to discover, nothing more for the pioneer to do, no romance of mystery in the world.

That great adventurer, Lawrence of Arabia, knew better than most men the Romance of the Unknown. Even in the later days when he was courting oblivion he wanted to share that romance, and explore the hitherto unvisited " empty desert " of southern Arabia. A letter, written in 1929, to Sir Hugh Trenchard,* betrays his eagerness : " Dear Sir Hugh, I knew you'd consider the Empty Desert idea. . . . It is the last piece of exploration on earth. Doing it completes our knowledge of the globe ". He was madly keen, and though nothing came of his suggestion to Sir Hugh, and he had no share in the exploration, he rejoiced in the romance of Bertram Thomas's marvellous journey. Writing to Edward Marsh, secretary to J. H. Thomas, he pours out his enthusiasm : " Bertram Thomas, our Agent at Muscat, has just crossed the Empty Quarter, that great desert of southern Arabia. It remained the only unknown corner of the world, and it is the end of the history of exploration. Thomas did it by camel, at his own expense. Every explorer for generations has dreamed of it. . . . I trust the imagination of J. H. T. (then Colonial Secretary) to understand your enthusiasm and mine for what is the finest geographical feat since Shackleton."

Since Bertram Thomas's triumph, the world has grown smaller. The geographical unknown is now, perhaps, confined to the upper reaches of the Amazon ; and they will soon yield their secrets to aviation. In other spheres of exploration limits have been reached. At one end of the scale of scientific investigation the microscope has reached limits of littleness ; at the other, the telescope has reached limits of bigness.

But neither microscope nor telescope can reveal *God as He is*. The most thrilling adventure of all is still left—the adventure of searching for reality, and being found by God.

* Now Lord Trenchard.

CHAPTER III

THE METHOD OF APPROACH

IT is no more possible to teach mysticism than it is to define it. My friend, Harry L. Hubbard, who was a genuine mystic, wrote a little book of practical instruction which he called *Self-training in Mysticism*. The title expresses just what is possible, no more, no less, as regards instruction in mysticism. It cannot be taught, like algebra or physical drill. The most that a mystic can do to help a potential mystic in the Way is to show him how he may train himself into readiness for whatever revelation or call may come to him. Progress in this matter is not so much by way of teaching, or even of guidance, as by way of development. It is a progress brought about by a stirring up of an inherent gift. By its very nature, mysticism is obliged to be self-supporting, for it is a direct approach to God, deriving from Him alone, and therefore only indirectly dependent on any human guidance or support.

Mysticism, on the subjective side, is a form of religious genius ; and genius can never be taught, it can at most be developed. Furthermore, the best development of genius is self-development, though useful help may come from outside. It must be remembered, also, that the popular conception of genius as being a sort of outstanding, intuitive ability in life's work narrows down the original meaning of the word, which is simply " the special inborn faculty of any individual ". That everyone has some special inborn faculty is, for mankind, one of the foundations of hope. Christians believe that every child of God is called to some special work in the world, and that by his genius, his special inborn faculty, he can do that work better than anyone else can ; for it is God who planned it for him, and calls

him to it.   Like all God's gifts, genius may be perverted to
unworthy and selfish uses.   We only personify it, and speak
of a man as " a genius " when he achieves something notable
by the right employment of his special inborn faculty.
Probably, too, it would be correct to add that the faculty
must itself be a notable one if it is to win for its possessor
(or possessed) the title of " a genius ", as the world employs
it.   It is only paradoxically and in exasperation that people
use the word in a disparaging sense, saying, for instance, of
some clumsy girl that " she has a genius for breaking
plates ".

The genius for religion which, in some manifestations, is
called mysticism, is expressed in many different ways.   For
self-training in mysticism it is essential to discover which way
is our way ;   that is to say, which manifestation is most
closely akin to the genius wherewith we are endowed.   No
one can train himself in a way entirely alien to his own
special inborn faculties.   That is my reason for devoting
the whole of Part II in this book to sketching, however
inadequately, the outlook and achievement of men and
women touched by the spirit of mysticism.   It is also my
reason for including in those sketches as great a variety as
possible of conscious and unconscious religious " geniuses ".
Mysticism is best learned through the impact of one living
soul upon another (whether living here or Beyond) ;   like
religion it is caught, not taught.   Fortunately, the great
mystics live again in their writings.   In one or other of the
mystical writers, greater or less, the earnest student can
discover the note with which his own higher self harmonises.
From them we get a message and an inspiration which
never die.

It is important that the net of our enquiry should be
cast as widely as possible, so as to include all who, in any
degree, are in harmony with our own particular genius of
religion, for it is from those with whom we are most in
harmony that we can learn most.   Some will find in Julian

of Norwich a kindred spirit ; others may derive more help
from Coventry Patmore, because they are of a more sophisticated temperament. As all are potential mystics, there
must be among the mystical writers at any rate one who
can strike the spark of sympathy in each one of the enquirers,
and so inspire the individual response.

Having emphasised the amazing variety of ways in
which the approach to God is made by the mystics, the next
step in our enquiry is to consider not their differences but
their likenesses. Are there any methods of approach upon
which they are all agreed ? To this question there is a
stirringly encouraging answer : all agree, explicitly or
implicitly, that the mystic approach to God is upward and
gradual. They recognise, of course, that " upward " is a
spatial synonym for what happens, and " gradual " is a
temporal synonym for how it happens. Human words must
always be inadequate to describe the working out of the
Divine purpose in infinity and eternity, but human words
are all we have to give expression to our own spiritual
experience.

The mystics, therefore, are content to speak and write
of an ascent. It may be an ascent of the Mount of Holiness
or of the Ladder of Perfection ; the actual terms matter
little. What does matter is that it implies climbing, striving,
reaching out after higher things. Secondly, they conceive
of this ascent as being made by stages, gradually. Moreover, they are agreed, almost unanimously, on the nature of
these stages, and their order ; though from the first it is
necessary to insist that their order is not a strictly consecutive
order. The stages overlap, and the striver can never boast
that he has permanently left behind any one of them. He
is forced to accept that simple saying, so abhorrent to human
pride, that " the life of every Christian is a series of fresh
beginnings ".

Bearing in mind this deeper and wider conception of
the mystic way, it may be said that for purposes of

enlightenment, the ascent can be thought of as consisting of three principal stages : the Purgative stage, the Illuminative stage, and the Unitive stage. On this all well-known mystical writers are agreed. Their interpretations of what the various stages mean, and what experiences mark each of them, do in many respects differ. But the general conception of an ascent by three stages is at the root of all accredited mystical writing on the method of the approach to God.

It must not be imagined that this conception is confined to the mystics, or that this method of approach is an exclusively mystical method. The whole argument of this book is meant to disprove the assumption of exclusiveness or monopoly on the part of any one of the three " elements of religion ", in defiance of the others. So it is not surprising to find that in the epitome of institutional and intellectual (or ethical) religion known as the Church Catechism, the three stages of the approach to God are recognised : the Purgative, that I should renounce the devil and all his works, the pomps and vanity of this wicked world, and all the sinful lusts of the flesh ; the Illuminative, that I should believe all the articles of the Christian faith ; the Unitive, that I should keep God's holy will and commandments and walk in the same all the days of my life. There is nothing far-fetched in this assimilation ; for in renunciation is to be found purgation, in faith is to be found illumination, and perfect obedience to God is of the essence of perfect union with Him.

Now consider how the religious genius of mysticism can help by revealing something of the inner meaning of this conception of the three stages, and how it can be a light on the path of simple folk in their approach to God.

(1) The purgative stage is the way of *liberation*, not merely the way of denial. Like all spiritual advance it is positive rather than negative. Too often, men picture to

themselves the fight against sin as a sort of surgical operation on the soul, the amputation of some invisible limb of their being. That is not S. John's conception of what he learned from his Master. *Whosoever committeth sin is the servant of sin.* The fight against sin is man's effort to escape, by God's grace, from the bondage and degradation in which sin enslaves him. Purgation is the *first step* to a fuller life. If we are to *run the race that is set before us*, it is requisite that we should *lay aside every weight and the sin which doth so easily beset us* (" doth closely cling to us ", like some stifling impediment).

It is important to lay stress on the negative side of sin, its hindrance of life, and its outcome in failure, because consciousness of sin usually concentrates at first on sins of the body—lust, greed, or violence. The consequence of this attitude is that because temptation comes through the body, there is ever present the tendency to blame the body, and to punish it as a proof of our hatred of sin. This is a mistake : it has no place in the Christian mystic's interpretation of the way of Purgation. For him there can be no hatred of the God-given body. Asceticism is not an end in itself. There is no trace of the heresy of Manicheism in true mysticism, no condemnation of the body as body. On the contrary, mysticism accepts the whole of the creation as being the gift of the Creator, to be used in His way and to His glory, here and hereafter : *Glorify God*, says S. Paul, *in your body and in your spirit, which are God's.*

It is the great work of the so-called " nature-mystics " that they proclaim this truth of the affinity between the whole of man and the whole of nature, since both are one in God. Not mutilation but sublimation must be the watchword ; for it is part of the purpose of God, who *shall fashion anew the body of our humiliation, that it may be conformed to the body of his glory, according to the working whereby he is able to subject all things unto himself.* (R.V.) It is not true, as the author of that beautifully mystical book, *The Roadmaker*, affirms, that " the great mystics, with all their insight and heavenly love, fell short when they sought freedom in complete separateness from creation, instead of perfect unity with it ". Nor is it a true description of the Christian mystics' attitude towards creation to declare, as some non-Christian mystics do, that " nature conceals God, but the supernatural in man reveals Him ". In this matter, as in so many others, the Christian mystic is saved from error by his loyalty to institutionalism and the Bible : he is assured that *the whole creation groaneth and travaileth in pain together until now. And not only they, but ourselves also, which have the first-fruits of the Spirit, even we ourselves groan within ourselves, waiting for the adoption, to wit, the redemption of our body.* At root, disparagement of the creation is disparagement of the Creator, who *saw everything that He had made, and, behold, it was very good :* it is also, as will be shown elsewhere, a misreading of the full meaning of the Incarnation.

The body, with its trials and temptations, looms large at the beginning of the purgative stage. There is a danger lest it should monopolise the wayfarer's whole attention. The consequences of such a one-sided outlook are disastrous ; first, because it causes the individual to overlook worse sins than those of the flesh, and secondly, because it engenders a false public opinion—a public opinion which condones grinding the faces of the poor while it condemns a lapse into drunkenness. " Purgation " means a good deal more than " signing the pledge ". It has always meant more. From the first, men and women have been assailed by temptations deeper than the temptations of bodily sensuality. " From the first ", for in the third chapter of Genesis there may be found as good a setting-out of the matter as any : *When the woman saw that the tree was good for food, and that it was pleasant to the eyes, and a tree to be desired to make one wise, she took of the fruit thereof, and did eat, and gave also to her husband with her.* This primeval passage unfolds the three principal lines of temptation : through the appe-

tites, " the tree was good for food ; through the senses,
" the tree was pleasant to the eyes " ; through the intellect,
" it was a tree to be desired to make one wise ".

✓ Temptations through the appetites assume a paramount
place in the pages of the Old Testament and of Divine
Lives of the Saints ; at any rate in the eyes of those who
read them with but little understanding of what may be
called more advanced forms of temptation. There is
always a danger lest, because carnal temptations are so
insurgent and universal, they should make men blind to the
more subtle temptations of æstheticism, the perverted love
of beauty and comfort which particularly marks the present
age. Men have come to hate the stark realities of life, and
suffering, and death ; they strive, with futile persistence, to
evade them or gloss them over. Consequently it has come
about that the spirit of man is corrupted by the conviction
that pain is worse than sin ; a conviction that is responsible
for the false sentiment which is producing an age of shirkers.
An example of this spirit of cowardly shirking is seen in the
resentment with which some people undergo the inevitable
hardships of married life and parenthood, and the short-
sighted cowardice with which they try to evade them. An
æstheticism which prefers a good figure to a full cradle is
decadent.

On the other hand, it is, I think, true to say that the
present age has, partly at any rate, grown out of that sin of
intellectual pride, that arrogance of rationalism, which
characterised the nineteenth century. The utter failure of
humanism is so apparent that no one of repute is foolish
enough to try to piece together its shattered shards, though
it is resurrected from time to time in freak disguises. Re-
verting to the fatal fruit of the tree, it is the second of the
three forms of temptation that has to be particularly taken
into account in our present enquiry into the approach to
God, and the hindrances to that approach. The false
æstheticism, so prevalent to-day, is not so much drawn

astray by the evil as " put off " by the good. In public worship, for example, and in other activities of institutional religion, it finds its senses offended by inadequate manners, inadequate music, inadequate ceremonial, inadequate architecture and ornament—above all, by inadequate agents—so that it condemns religion because it finds religious people and religious practices imperfect ; yet protesting all the time that it would be deeply religious if religious observances satisfied its senses. No one can deny that there is much to offend (some of the offences in public worship are considered in a later chapter), but the fact that the Divine image is imperfectly presented by human agents and material means is no excuse whatsoever for by-passing God.

Before going on to consider the difficulties and the opportunities of the illuminative stage in the mystic's approach to God, it is necessary to remind ourselves of some general truths which apply to the first stage, as well as to further stages. Everyone should know, for instance, that temptation is not sin. Yet there are thousands of earnest souls who are made miserable by their failure to keep in mind this elementary truth of the spiritual life. They worry themselves into a fever of despair, because they are tempted—by wandering thoughts, or lascivious desires, or stresses of irritability—not remembering the courage-inspiring assurance that so long as they do not give in, so long as the will-to-good remains inviolate, they are not guilty.

When they do give in, and incur guilt, there is only one road to restoration. It is an infallible road—the way of repentance. Here again, it is easy to be side-tracked by popular misconceptions, so that it is wise to remind ourselves, over and over again, of the old, simple truths, or to refresh our understanding by turning to the writings of the mystics about the method of purgation. Repentance, in its Christian meaning is not resentment at our own failure, nor annoyance with ourselves at our weakness, nor the humiliation which comes from being found out in wrong-doing. It is a dynamic

change of heart (μετάνοια), and has three essential conditions, as we were taught, or should have been taught, in
our childhood. There must be sorrow for the past, because
sin is an offence against love, not merely because it humili-
ates the sinner. There must be acknowledgment in the
present, our tribute to truth : *If we confess our sins, He is
faithful and just to forgive us our sins, and to cleanse us from all
unrighteousness.* There is no forgiveness for those who do
not seek it ; God never *forces* His gifts upon us. Thirdly,
the dynamic nature of repentance is proved by a firm
purpose of amendment ; it is our tribute to righteousness,.
without which penitence and confession are unreal.

To give an illustration of how these simple truths of the
spiritual life may have a fresh light thrown upon them from
the angle of mysticism ; the most notable mystic I have
ever met once said to me, " I can never make up my mind
whether I ought to make my Confession in preparation
for my Communion, or my Communion in preparation for
my Confession." There was nothing deliberately whimsical
about this remark. As he explained, what he meant was
that in Communion he was conscious of so close a fellowship
with the Saviour that he shared not only His burning hatred
for sin, but also in some measure His penetrating insight to
recognise and eradicate the disease of sin, hidden as it so
often is by its own symptoms. This mystical suggestion is
not necessarily recommended as a regular devotional
practice, but it enshrines a truth which may well help
towards a worthier repentance. A deeper emotion and a
more carefully directed sincerity are the fruits of penitence
for which a Christian craves ; they can only be learned in
their fullness from the Friend of Sinners.

All through the purgative stage of its pilgrimage, it is
obvious that the soul needs the help of institutional religion
to order, discipline, and direct mystical experience. That
consciousness of a change of mind which is Christian repentance is so revolutionary an experience that the soul

tends to look upon it as a thing distinct, final and complete. The Church, with age-long wisdom, corrects this assumption by providing a form of confession in all her regular services of public worship, thus emphasising the important truth that repentance is a state, not merely an incident of life. This is just one instance of the stabilising influence of institutional religion, as it curbs the exaggerated trust in spasmodic experiences which is liable to lead the mystic astray. There are plenty of other instances of the benefit which accompanies a humble recognition of the Church's code of discipline. There is, above all, the comfort of an external, authoritative message of forgiveness bestowed upon the penitent sinner, by Divine direction, from the Head through the Body. No permanent satisfaction is to be found in the falsely comforting assurance, " Every man his own absolver ".

Having considered some aspects of the purgative stage in the approach to God, we begin instinctively to ask ourselves, " Is there any test of my progress in this part of the mystical ascent, any criterion of advance ; or is the soul lost in a maze of recurrent temptation, finding no outlet, and reaching no goal ? " If such were the case, the way of the mystic would be not only hard but hopeless. Perseverance without hope is impossible. That is why God, who calls us to perseverance, never fails to provide us with hope, even though we scarcely recognise it at times. His way is the way of hope, going on from strength to strength, along a hard road but a road marked by milestones of achievement. One achievement of purgation—perhaps the most notable, and in some ways the most practical—which marks a milestone of advance in the approach to God is to be found in what S. Ignatius Loyola calls "*Indifference to Creatures*". This is the climax of the purgative stage, as well as the starting point for the higher peaks of mysticism. No one has expressed the truth of this matter, and its setting in the wider purpose of God, better than Ignatius himself. His words should be imprinted on the heart of every aspirant :

Man was created to praise, reverence, and serve God our Lord, and by this means to save his soul ; and the other things on the face of the earth were created for man's sake, and in order to aid him in the prosecution of the end for which he was created. Whence it follows, that a man ought to make use of them just so far as they help him to attain his end, and that he ought to withdraw himself from them just so far as they hinder him. It is therefore necessary that we should make ourselves indifferent to all created things, in all that is left to the liberty of our free-will, and is not forbidden ; in such sort that we do not for our part wish for health rather than sickness, for wealth rather than poverty, for honour rather than dishonour, for a long life rather than a short one, and so in all other things, desiring and choosing only that which may lead us more directly to the end for which we were created.

Two facts about this indifference should be specially noted. First, that Ignatius does not order what is impossible, that we should not feel attracted or repelled by created things ; for that would mean that we ceased to be human. He says we are to make ourselves *indifferent ;* that is to say, we are to overcome our natural impulses, and so discipline them as to be able to act with perfect freedom in the service of God. Secondly, indifference may be of two kinds ; indifference of sensibility (the result of sloth, or callousness, or subnormality), and indifference of the will. It is this last alone which Ignatius requires. As W. H. Longridge points out in his book on the *Exercises of S. Ignatius Loyola* from which this paragraph borrows,[6] the more modern word " detachment " expresses a large part of what Ignatius means by indifference, but not quite the whole. One might add that the revisers of the Prayer Book by substituting " impartially " for " indifferently " in the Prayer for the Church have not found the completely right word. " Impartiality " will not do. " Detachment " will not do. It is best to stick to the expression *Indifference* to *Creatures*, and meditate upon it until we understand it, and, by God's grace, experience it. Indifference to creatures is a very happy state of freedom in which to manifest power, as the saints have shown. For they exhibit in their lives that freedom from dependence on any mundane base, and all that self-confidence of spiritual fitness, which rightly characterise a Christian commando.

(2) The soul does not pass out of the purgative into the illuminative stage as a man passes out of one room into another, *shutting the door after him*. In this life, the world and the flesh are always threatening the integrity of the soul, even when it has made some considerable advance in the mystic ascent, and has experienced some degree of illumination, or had some foretaste of the highest unitive stage. *There is no discharge in that war :* to relax is to court disaster. Nevertheless, the experiences of the illuminative stage are different from those of the purgative stage, even when they are simultaneous with them.

Perhaps the simplest way to understand the difference is to examine the meaning of the expression " self-denial " ; remembering the words of the Master, *If any man will come after Me, let him deny himself*, and acknowledging that self-denial is a key-stone of the Christian life. In the purgative stage, a Christian will interpret " self-denial " as meaning the denial of certain things to self ; both things wrong in themselves, and things which though harmless in themselves are relinquished from some good motive, the good being superseded by the better. The Christian duty of fasting springs to mind in thinking of this kind of self-denial : it is a step towards the purgative ideal of indifference to creatures. In the illuminative stage, however, the soul discovers the deeper truth that self-denial means denial *of* self more truly than denial *to* self. Self-will is revealed as the supreme temptation to be fought. The attitude to which the soul is brought in the illuminative stage is expressed in the prayer :

O my God, I am not my own but Thine :
Take me for Thy own :
Make me in all things to do Thy holy will.
O my God, I give myself to Thee : . . .
Make me and keep me Thine.

" Self-sacrifice " is, I think, a better term than self-denial, because it has a more positive implication. Nevertheless it is open to the same two degrees of interpretation : it may mean the sacrifice of self for others, as when we speak of those who have made the " supreme sacrifice " of war, in laying down their lives for others. This is a quality which varies as times and circumstances and stimuli vary. The man who is wrought up to a high pitch of self-sacrifice in war may show himself a laggard in self-sacrifice when peace comes. The only permanent basis of self-sacrifice—what makes self-sacrifice an integral part of a man's nature—is that self-dedication to God which gives all to gain all, and which asks only to be used. The man who has thus sacrificed self to God will never fail, in peace or war, on the appeal of friends, *or of enemies*, to give himself—his whole self —to those who need him. It is his taking of the Cross, his sharing in the perfect act of self-sacrifice which the Saviour alone could make. The bond between self-dedication to God and Christian self-sacrifice is unbreakable. This is the revelation which comes to a mystic chiefly in the second stage of his progress. It is summed up, in its devotional aspect, by Thomas à Kempis in his hauntingly beautiful phrase, " Love all for Jesus ; but Jesus for Himself ".

Just as the temptations of the two first stages in mysticism differ from one another, so the ideals which are envisaged differ. The ideal of the purgative stage might be called " the life of righteousness " ; the ideal of the illuminative stage, " the life of holiness ". The latter implies a concentration of all the faculties, will, intellect, and feeling, upon God. And the greatest of these is will. It is because the soul has attained to some vision of God, and has received illumination in the way, that this second stage marks an advance. The dedication of self to God is a higher achievement than the dedication of external works to Him. It is in this respect that the difference between righteousness and holiness is exemplified.

One consideration of outstanding importance needs to be taken into account, namely, that if self-sacrifice is to be acceptable to God the self that we sacrifice must be worth offering. Self-development is a part of our duty of self-dedication. The popular opinion that self-denying and self-sacrificing people are weak, emasculate, lacking in vitality and personality, must be exposed as one of the Devil's lies. It is the strong men, the men who are capable of sinning *as it were with a cart-rope* whose self-emptying into the abyss of God's dynamic love counts for most with God. It is the Simon Peters, the Augustins, who swell the credit balance, not the weak creatures who simply accept the will of another because they have no will of their own. Such weaklings can offer nothing, since they have nothing to offer.

For the strong, who have to be broken, not bent, the way of illumination is usually a grim journey through the shades. The experience of dereliction, of being forsaken by God, very often accompanies the development of the illuminative life. Some account of it will be given in the lives and writings of typical mystics sketched in subsequent chapters. The only point that it is necessary to make here is that this " Dark Night of the Soul " is nothing unnatural or abnormal. It is what might be expected when the eyes of sinful man are opened to the illumination of God's holiness : *I have heard of Thee by the hearing of the ear : but now mine eye seeth Thee. Wherefore I abhor myself, and repent in dust and ashes.* As the bodily eye is dazzled and tortured when gazing directly into the sun's rays, so the eye of the soul is at first darkened by the blinding brilliance of the nearer vision of God. As the illumination grows, the mystic can only pray :

O help us to see
'Tis only the splendour of light hideth Thee.

The goal of his quest is hidden in the light of its own glory.

The means by which, from the human side, this stage of illumination is reached is meditation, in its many aspects and degrees. The whole subject of meditation and its connection with contemplation is dealt with in many treatises of a more or less technical nature. All that need be said here is that meditation may be described as " listening to God ", whereas contemplation is waiting upon God in silent and utter receptivity. In meditation there is not the same completeness of self-forgetfulness that there is in contemplation. Both these terms, however, are used with considerable elasticity of meaning by different writers ; some making them simply two steps in the same experience, while others seem to identify contemplation with the consummation of mystical experience in the third stage of the ascent. The attempt to define or circumscribe them only results in a misunderstanding of two methods of approach to God which merge into one another, because they are conditioned by the same need for grace, grace which can only come from one Source.

(3) The Unitive stage takes us into the realm of the ineffable. For those who have not experienced it any attempt at description would be an act of presumption. Even the greatest of mystics admit their inability to find words to express what they have experienced. They use figures of speech, but acknowledge that they convey no adequate or even recognisable account of what has been shown to them. When we come to consider what they have recorded we shall find ourselves confronted with a dark and impenetrable mystery. None the less, because it is the climax of the mystical ascent and the logical outcome of the

spiritual approach to God, we shall examine with gratitude the fragmentary hints by which men like Richard Rolle pierce the darkness with some faint gleam of enlightenment.

It must be pointed out, however, that though some of the mystical writers, whose outlook we are to consider in the next few chapters, have made the full ascent, this is not true of all of them.   They are chosen as witnesses to the mystical spirit, not as supreme mystics.   Some of them, indeed, cannot be called " mystics " in any technical sense of that word.   But all are animated and conditioned, in some degree, by the mystical standard of values : in the variety of their expression they help towards an understanding of the wide-spread, unifying force of this inward experience of first-hand religion.

THE EARLY ENGLISH MYSTICS

THE white star of mysticism was at its zenith in the fourteenth century. Its pure ray shone through the clouds of corruption, war and pestilence, which overshadowed the countries of Europe. In Italy the corruption of the Papacy failed to stifle the new spirit of simple Christianity which marked the early days of the Franciscan movement, though Francis himself had died a hundred years before. In the Low Countries and in Germany, ravaged though they were by constant war, a glowing spiritual light was kindled by the writings of Blessed John Ruysbroeck (1293-1381), Eckhard, Suso, Tauler, and others. The great Spanish mystics were of a later date.

In England, too, mysticism reached its highest pitch of illumination in the fourteenth century, which gave us the writings of Richard Rolle of Hampole (born about 1290), Walter Hilton (died 1396), and Dame Julian of Norwich (died about 1442), three notable contemporaries. It was also the century in which Margery Kempe lived, and in which an anonymous author produced one of the most outstanding mystical treatises, *The Cloud of Unknowing*. In the century before, Bishop Richard Poore (?) had written his book of spiritual instruction, *The Ancren Riwle*, for the three sister anchoresses at Tarrant Keynston in Dorset. It was a time of rich spiritual flowering, perhaps the richest in the history of the Church since the days of the Apostles.

This wonderful illumination shone all the brighter for the blackness of its background. Throughout the period when these writers flourished England was drained of manhood and wealth by never-ending wars ; and, far worse, the plague of the Black Death, which appeared first in 1348, carried off more than half the population before the end of the century. Tribulation and anguish stalked the kingdom. The French wars, glorified by later historians, were in fact filibustering expeditions. Crécy and Poitiers were successful skirmishes won by the use of a new technique of warfare, backed by the stedfastness of the English archers who exploited it. Edward III may have believed in his dynastic claims to portions of France (for a king can believe anything, so artificial is the atmosphere of adulation in which he is brought up), but those who followed him to battle were actuated more by the lust of booty and conquest than by any thoughts of the rights or wrongs of inheritance. In the words of Froissart, " The English will never love or honour their king unless he be victorious and a lover of arms and war against their neighbours, and especially such as are greater and richer than themselves ". They supported Edward III, and made a hero of him, not because his wars were just but because they were successful. Military victories abroad gilded the pill of abject poverty at home, a poverty due in no small measure to the expense of war ; in itself a national defeat.

Far more important things were, however, happening at home than on the petty battlefields of France. It was a century of social upheaval, unequalled until the coming of the Industrial Revolution five centuries later. The immediate cause of this upheaval was the Black Death. By carrying off half the labourers of the country it enhanced the value of the survivors. They found that they were wanted, badly wanted ; and they began to make their own terms. Not without violence, some of the traditional barriers of class-distinction were broken down. The Feudal System began to totter. The Peasant Revolt of 1380 was but a symptom of a wide-spread unrest. Some of the new-born social aspirations were expressed in the *Vision of Piers the Plowman*. The gentler and more humane aspect of the movement can be discovered in Chaucer's poetry. Men were, as they are to-day, " on their toes " to spring into a new world.

The Church, as to-day, was involved in these social and industrial changes. She had also her own peculiar anxieties ; for the spirit of unrest permeated the religious as well as the secular life of the nation. Wyclif, whether right or wrong in his controversial activities, succeeded at any rate in making men think, and thought has an explosive force in the lives of those who are not used to it. By the end of the century, Lollardism had so swept the country that frightened members of the orthodox party exclaimed that half the people of England were followers of Wyclif. The measure of their exaggeration was perhaps the measure of their fear.

On these stormy waters was poured the oil of mysticism. It saved the ship of the Church (and possibly the State) from wreck. For it is not by a change of method but by a change of mind that true spiritual revival is brought about ; and without spiritual revival there can be no permanent improvement in social or industrial life. It is by bringing men into a fresh relationship with the infinite and the eternal that they are made fit to pursue a right course amid the changes and chances of this fleeting world. It has always been the strength and the justification of mysticism that it has provided this stabilising force, centring men's thoughts on God's eternal changelessness, conforming their wills to His eternal purpose of love. Mysticism to-day has precisely the same function to perform, and the same saving grace to perform it, that it had in the days of the early English mystics.

Their influence was undoubtedly very great ; far greater than most secular historians recognise. The writings of Walter Hilton, for instance, were read in manuscript by large numbers of people, and his teaching was spread through word of mouth by his readers. His chief book, *The Scale of Perfection*, was a favourite book with the King's

mother ; and it seems to have been eagerly read by rich
and poor, learned and unlearned.   It opened men's minds
to a truer standard of values than the political and military
leaders could know.   Such opening of the mind is, in itself,
a revolution.

Englishmen can claim, with well-warranted pride, that
their nation has produced a band of mystical writers who
are second to none.   Some book-students of mysticism may
be more impressed by the sirocco of devotional passion which
scorched the souls of the great Spanish mystics ; others feel
the fascination of that darkling obscurity in which some of
the Teutonic mystics veiled the record of their experiences,
and of their musings ; but for sheer simplicity of truth, and
homeliness of love, the English mystics of the fourteenth
century are, to my mind, supreme.

Primus inter pares, first among equals, stands Walter
Hilton—not first in time, but first in appeal.   He saw life
whole, and he wrote for all sorts and conditions of men,
with that blunt common sense in matters spiritual which is
so acceptable to the English temperament.   Men felt in
their hearts " he is one of us ".   He was not, in any technical
sense, a recluse ; nor did he belong to one of the stricter
religious Orders.   He mixed among men.   Yet his life, as
an Augustinian canon in the priory of Thurgarton near
Nottingham, must have been simple and secluded.   In that
quiet spot where the rolling uplands of Sherwood Forest
merge into the Lincolnshire plain, and a tiny stream flows
by the priory walls to join the Trent two miles below, it is
easy to imagine that there was little to disturb the contemplative life, if a man's heart was set upon it.   On the other
hand, the Thurgarton community was a large one, and the
whole neighbourhood was in the possession and under the
management of the priory.   The canons were, in the best
sense, business men, men of their time and place, as well as
servants of the eternal God.   So it is no wonder to find
that Hilton's writing is brightened by a gentle humour and

a quaint love for the practical, which appeals by virtue of its humanity. Hilton was not of the world ; but he was certainly in it : and he was not ashamed to be in it. He had that essential and timeless link, sympathy, which has enabled him for more than five centuries to comfort, encourage, and guide wayfarers in the world ; men and women who would fain be not of the world, but look for *a city which hath foundations, whose builder and maker is God.* He stands, therefore, above a number of mystical writers, even those of the highest rank in their particular enclave, who seem to have almost forgotten the grace of sympathy. Their inspiration lacks the fulcrum of *sharing ;* somehow they have missed the full implications of the Incarnation.

I am, therefore, prepared to shock most students of mysticism by expressing the opinion that Hilton was a fuller Christian than his predecessor Richard Rolle, that supremely gifted pioneer of English mysticism ; or even that William Law was a fuller Christian than his master Jacob Boehme. Concentration is not the same thing as consecration. One man may be the greater mystic and the other the greater saint. There is every reason to suppose that Rolle had deeper mystical experiences than Hilton. He received more ; but did he give more ? That is the question. Fullness of experience must always be matched by fullness of expression. Christians get to give. No disparagement of Rolle is here suggested by this query about the fullness of his giving. He gave to the best of his ability. What must be taken into consideration is the possibility that the higher an aspirant is rapt into the realm of the ineffable, the more loath he may be to return. And when, against his will, he is brought back by what seems to be some trivial earthly claim (" It's your turn to wash up ") he may be jarred into irritability. There is a tradition that even Rolle, at one time, was irritable. I have known modern mystics who showed the same incongruity of conduct. They were so intent on the vision of the glorified Christ that they forgot Jesus the Carpenter, and the homely message of helpfulness and human affection inherent in the truth of the Incarnation.

Walter Hilton's chief contribution towards the understanding of the mystical way of life is his orderly setting forth of the three modes in which a Christian may serve his God :

"Thou must understand that God is served by three kinds of life, as either by an active life, or by a contemplative, or by a third, that is mixed of them both, and therefore is commonly called a mixed life.

"(1) The Active Life belongeth to worldly men and women that are gross and ignorant as to the understanding or knowledge of ghostly works or ways, for they neither feel nor taste devotion by fervour of love as other men do, nor may they well conceive what it is or how it may be come by ; nevertheless they have in them the fear of God and of the pains of Hell, and therefore they eschew and forbear sin, and have a desire for to please God, and to attain to Heaven, and a good will they bear to their Christian brethren.

"(2) The Contemplative Life consisteth in perfect love and charity, felt inwardly by spiritual virtues ; and by the soothfast knowing and sight of God. . . . As perfect Contemplation as can be had in this life lieth both in cognition and affection ; that is to say, in knowing and in perfect loving of God. And that is when a man's soul is first reformed by fullhead of virtues to the image of Jesus. And afterwards, when it pleaseth God to visit him, he is taken in from all earthly and fleshly affections, from vain thoughts and imaginings of all bodily creatures, and, as it were, much ravished out of bodily wits, and then by the grace of the Holy Ghost is illumined to see by understanding soothfastness itself, which is God, and ghostly things, with a soft, sweet, burning love in Him, so perfectly that he ravisheth of His love, and so he is oned with God, and conformed to the image of the Trinity.

"(3) The Mixed Life belongeth to Prelates of Holy Church and to pastors and curates who have charge and superiority over other men and women, for to teach and govern them, both as to their bodies and as to their souls, and principally to animate and guide them in the performance of the deeds of mercy both corporal and spiritual towards their Christian brethren. Also this mixed life appertaineth to some temporal men, who are owners of much land and goods and have withal some dominion and mastership over other men. For if these men having such external charge and cares lying on them, out of some obligation or necessity, would altogether leave or neglect such charge and businesses of the world pertaining to them, and give themselves wholly to the exercises of contemplative life, they would not do well in so doing, for they observe not the order of charity. This mixed life did our Lord Himself exercise, and show in the same manner, for an example to all other men that have taken on them the state or condition that requireth the exercises of the said mixed life, that is to say, that they should sometimes apply themselves to the external affairs and businesses belonging to their charge, and to the curing of such their Christian brethren as pertain to them to look to, instruct or provide for ; and this to do according to reason and discretion and their need ; and at another time to give themselves to devotion and to the exercises of a Contemplative life, being principally reading and praying."

How relevant all this is to the needs and circumstances of the present time becomes clear in the further reading of this most practical of all great mystics, so trustworthy and strong by Divine inspiration and human sympathy.

Turning once again to the thought of the three stages in the mystical ascent to God, it is from Richard Rolle that most can be learned about the unitive stage. That he did experience the complete *one-ing* with the One, on several occasions, is a certain fact. But his attempt to describe it falls far short of the reality. The three descriptive words that he uses are *canor*, *calor*, and *dulcor*—song, heat, and sweetness :

" In these three that are tokens of most perfect love, the highest perfection of Christian religion without all doubt is found ; and I have now, Jesu granting, received these three after the littleness of my capacity. Nevertheless I dare not make myself even to the saints that have shone in them, for they peradventure have received them more perfectly. Yet shall I be busy in virtue that I may more burningly love, more sweetly sing, and more plenteously feel the sweetness of love."

These three are, as he says, " tokens of love ". But it is in love itself that true unity is to be found. He sums up his experience and his philosophy, his devotion and his life-aim, in a beautiful passage :

" Love is a burning yearning after God with a wonderful delight and certainty. God is light and burning ; light clarifies our reason, burning kindles our desires, that we desire naught but Him. Love is a life, coupling together the loving and the loved. For Meekness makes us sweet to God ; Purity joins us to God ; Love makes us one with God. Love is the beauty of all virtues. Love is the thing through which God loves us and we God, and each one of us another. Love is the desire of the heart ay thinking til him that it loves ; and when it has that it loves, then it joys and nothing can make it sorry. Love is yearning between two, with lastingness of thought, Love is a stirring of the soul for to love God for Himself. and all other things for God ; the which love when it is ordained in God, it does away all inordinate love in anything that is not good. But all deadly sin is inordinate love for a thing that is naught ; then love puts out all deadly sin. Love is a virtue which is the rightest affection of a man's soul. Truth may be without love, but it cannot help without it. Love is perfection of letters, virtue of prophecy ; fruit of truth, help of sacraments ; stabiling of wit and knowledge ; riches of poor men, life of dying men. See how good love is ! "

Here is the perfection of mysticism. Nothing higher can be reached, in this life, by the individual seeker. Nevertheless, the question may be raised whether the perfection of mysticism is, in truth, the perfection of life. Are all other activities of the soul mere handmaids of loving contemplation ? Is the body a clog or an instrument in true living ? Hilton supplies the convincing answer, " This *mixed* life did our Lord in Himself exercise ". He had his times of perfect contemplation, but not to the exclusion of the perfect activity of His ministry to others. He was the ever-ready servant of all, and *He never resented an interruption* (what an example and a warning to the devotionally-minded introvert, masquerading as a mystic !). Christians can only have one Model. In the life of Jesus they find that spur to " social service " in its widest and best sense, without which religion is barren, like the barrenness of some pure, cold mountain top. The mysticism which is essential to human needs, in the present as in the past, is an understanding approach to a God who says, as Joseph said of old, *Ye shall not see my face, except your brother be with you.* There is no such thing as an *individual* Christian. The religion which is " a matter between myself and God " has its attraction for certain temperaments, but it is not Christianity, nor is it true mysticism. If mysticism is to play its part in the uplift of the world it must be purged of all egotism.

Lady Julian of Norwich, most perfect of mystics, is a shining example of one whose intensity of personal devotion never obscured for a moment her love for her *even-Christians.* Her evangelical spirit refused to be separated from them ; for she knew that she could not be like her Saviour unless she bore, in some degree, the sin of the world. She could claim, with S. Paul, that she was one *who now rejoice in my sufferings for you, and fill up that which is behind of the afflictions of Christ in my flesh for His body's sake, which is the Church.* For a true follower of Christ, as Lady Julian was, there is no rest and no peace so long as sin reigns in the world. The sins of others were as great a burden to her as her own :

"The soul that willeth to be in rest when another man's sin cometh to mind, he shall flee it as the pain of hell, seeking unto God for remedy, for help against it. For the beholding of other man's sins, it maketh as it were a thick mist afore the eyes of the soul, and we cannot, for the time, see the fairness of God, but if we may behold them with contrition with him, with compassion on him, and with holy desire to God for him. For without this it harmeth and tempesteth and hindereth the soul that beholdeth them. For this I understood in the Shewing of Compassion."

This depth of sympathy was matched in her soul by depth of spiritual insight into ultimate truth. Julian describes herself as " a simple creature that could no letter " ; which does not mean that she was illiterate. She made no claims to theological learning : it was the mystical more than the intellectual element in religion which brought her to an understanding of holy mysteries. She wrote *not in the words which man's wisdom teacheth, but which the Holy Ghost teacheth ; comparing spiritual things with spiritual* (" interpreting spiritual things to spiritual men "—R. V. Margin). With love for a key she was able to unlock the inner chambers of Divine revelation. Many philosophers and theologians have written about the universality of God, or about monism in its various interpretations ; but none of them, in all their tortuous approaches, has got deeper down to the root of the matter than this humble, child-like anchoress, making the direct approach through mystical experience and first-hand religion :

"After this I saw God in a Point, that is to say in mine understanding,—by which sight I saw that He is in all things. . . . For I saw truly that God doeth all-thing, be it never so little. And I saw truly that nothing is done by hap nor by adventure, but all things by the fore-seeing wisdom of God : if it be hap or adventure in the sight of man, our blindness and our unforesight is the cause. For the things that are in the foreseeing wisdom of God from without beginning (which rightfully and worshipfully and continually He leadeth to the best end) as they come about fall to us suddenly, ourselves unwitting ; and thus by our blindness and our unforesight we say : these be haps and adventures. But to our Lord God they be not so. Wherefore me behoveth needs to grant that all-thing is done, it is well-done ; for our Lord God doeth all. For in this time the working of creatures was not shewed, but the working of our Lord God in the creature : for He is in the Mid-point of all thing, and all he doeth. . . . And thus, as much as might be for the time, the rightfulness of God's working was shewed to the soul."

There is no trace of pantheism in this passage. Dame Julian and her two great contemporaries, Rolle and Hilton, were preserved from that snare by which so many mystical writers have been trapped. The Man Jesus was their familiar friend, as truly as the Glorified Christ was the object of their profoundest adoration : they were neither monophysites nor pantheists ; for none knew better than they that :

> We may not climb the heavenly steeps
> To bring the Lord Christ down ;
> In vain we search the lowest deeps,
> For him no depths can drown ;
> But warm, sweet, tender, even yet
> A present help is he ;
> And faith has still its Olivet,
> And love its Galilee.

In this balanced attitude of service and devotion they were ordered and maintained by their loyalty to the institutional fellowship into which they had been born at baptism, and in which they lived supported by the heavenly nourishment of the Body broken and the Blood shed. Julian reached heights of vision which perhaps no mystic has surpassed ; but from her may be learned that loyalty to institutionalism which was a fundamental quality of all the early English mystics.   Rolle or Hilton or Poore or the author of *The Cloud of Unknowing* might just as well have written her glowing words :

" For one single person may oftentimes be broken, but the whole body of Holy Church was never broken, nor ever shall be, without end.   And therefore a sure thing it is, a good and a gracious, ιο will meekly and mightily to be fastened to our Mother, Holy Church, that is Christ Jesus.   For the Food of Mercy that is His dear-worthy blood and precious water is plenteous to make us fair and clean ; the sweet gracious hands of our Mother be ready and diligently about us.   For He in all this working useth the office of a kind nurse that hath not else to do but to entend about the salvation of her child."

In that conviction, just as much as in the revival of the inward spirituality of the mystical way, lies the hope of the future.   For one cannot live and bear fruit without the other.

CHAPTER V

MYSTICISM IN PROSE

IN order to understand and appreciate the early English mystics we find it necessary to learn their language, and to try to project on to the screen of our imagination something of their outlook, so different from ours. This difficulty does not arise when we turn to Thomas à Kempis. He is a man of no period, or of all—" for all times, and for all people " ; that is, a Catholic pure and simple. So he is a fitting link between the early mystics and those later writers whose mystical language and outlook are more familiar to us. It is true he was not an Englishman by birth or residence ; but just as he was of no time, so he was beyond nationality. Readers as different from one another as Ignatius Loyola and George Eliot responded to his attraction and his influence.

This universality of appeal is all the more remarkable when we consider how narrow were the bounds of his outward life : like Walter Hilton, he was a Canon Regular of the Order of S. Augustin, but his exterior life was much more circumscribed than Hilton's. His outlook was definitely the outlook of a monk. He spent the greater part of his life in a Community, though he was not ordained priest until 1413, being then thirty-three years of age. The account of his death may still be read in the Chronicle of Agnetenberg, the priory in which he served for seventy-two years :

" In the same year (1471) on the feast of S. James the Less, after Compline, died our dearly loved Brother Thomas Haemerken, born at Kempen, a town in the diocese of Cologne. He was in the ninety-second year of his age, the sixty-third [it was really the sixty-fifth] of his religious clothing, and the fifty-eighth of his priesthood. In his youth he was a disciple, at Deventer, of Master Florentius, who sent him to his [Thomas's] brother, who was then Prior of Agnetenberg.   He was then twenty years of age ; he received the habit from his brother after six years' probation, and throughout his monastic life he underwent great poverty, temptations, and labours. He copied our Bible and many other books, some for the use of the convent, and others for sale.   Further, for the edification of the young he composed divers small treatises in a plain and simple style, but full of wisdom and practical utility.   He had a special devotion to the Passion of our Lord, and excelled as a comforter of the tempted and distressed.   At length, in his old age, after suffering from dropsy of the legs, he fell asleep in the Lord.   He was buried in the East Cloister, by the side of Brother Peter Herbert."

His favourite motto is said to have been, " I sought for rest, but found it not save in a little corner with a little book."

Here, then, was a man who shunned the world, who would neither be in it or of it.   How is it that he could produce a book second only to the Bible as a spiritual guide and comforter for men of every variety of theological standpoint, Catholics and Protestants, and even those who have no settled standpoint at all, questing agnostics ?   It is one of the wonders in the spiritual history of mankind that this book, *The Imitation of Christ*, never seems to grow old, and never seems out-of-place.   Among men of good will its appeal is almost universal.   Volumes might be written to try to explain the secret of its influence.   Possibly, the root-explanation lies in its utter naturalness, heart speaking to heart.   Thomas, the imitator of Christ, just tells the story of his own inner life, without a trace of self-consciousness, or priggishness, or pedagogy.   He is entirely natural, humble, and honest with himself.   Moreover, he offers his book to his fellow Christians simply because he loves them ; and for no other reason.   It is a kind of self-giving, so complete that it cannot fail to win response ; and it has never failed to win response for nearly five hundred years. It is as fresh to-day as it was when it was first written, steeped as it is in eternity.

It may rightly be said that *The Imitation of Christ* is devotional rather than mystical. But devotion and mysticism are not rivals, or mutually exclusive ; they are branches of the same stem. If not technically a mystic, Thomas à Kempis cannot be omitted from any account of religious writers who have illustrated in their lives and writings the working of the spirit of mysticism. The true judgment in this matter, as it seems to me, has been delivered by Fr. Sharpe (in his book, *Mysticism : its Nature and Value*), so admirably, that it must be quoted without addition, and without subtraction :

" The Imitation of Christ . . . probably owes much of its vast popularity to its constant recurrence to the elementary duties of religion and morality, and its insistence on the necessity of their performance as the prerequisite of the more exalted spiritual states. The 'purgative ', 'illuminative ', and 'unitive ' ways are seen, so to speak, together, and are dealt with as aspects or constituents of the Christian life as a whole, to the completeness of which all three are necessary and, in different ways, of equal importance. The purely mystical passages are comparatively few and short ; and the abundance of practical directions the book contains has sometimes caused its mystical character to be entirely overlooked. This disproportion, however, is quite sufficiently to be accounted for by the character of the work, which is that of a directory of spiritual life in general, and not a scientific treatise on any particular department of it. In such a book any attempts at describing the indescribable phenomena of mysticism would obviously have been out of place, whereas the practical details of the lower and preliminary states admit of and require minute explanation. But the tone of the whole book is

mystical, and the most commonplace duties and the most
humiliating strivings with temptation are in a manner
illuminated and glorified by the brilliancy of the result
to which they tend. Thus, in point of fact, the higher
and lower elements, the mystical and the non-mystical,
the purgative, the illuminative, and the unitive, are
blended in actual human experience." [7]

Thomas à Kempis' " constant recurrence to the elementary duties of religion and morality " not only enhances his
attractiveness to the English temperament, which ever
emphasises " practical " religion, it also makes him a con-
necting link between mystical directors like Richard Poore
and Walter Hilton and later writers, like William Law, who
found divinity in Duty. So to William Law we turn as
representing an aspect of mysticism which is specially
illustrative of its meaning for Englishmen.

His reputation and fame have been below his deserts,
because he is chiefly known by one book, *A Serious Call to
a Devout and Holy Life*, which is probably not his greatest,
and deals almost exclusively with the intellectual or (more
obviously) the ethical element in religion. It is one of the
masterpieces of moral literature, as distinct (if it can be
distinct) from devotional literature. But it only exhibits one
side of Law's genius. Another side appears in his controversial pamphlets, which are not only supremely good in
matter and manner, but are also evidence of the close
connection between the intellectual and the ethical, and an
exposure of the barrenness of the intellectual divorced from
the ethical. So, too, from the other point of view, as
for instance in his *Letters to the Bishop of Bangor*, Law
makes plain, in burning words, that intellectual honesty is
ethical integrity ; and in proving his adversary guilty of
non sequiturs he proves him guilty of sin.

These two specimens of Law's work, models in their
clarity, have tended to obscure the third and most remarkable product of his genius, *The Spirit of Prayer*, which must

be classed among the most notable of English mystical writings. There is also his less original book, *The Way of Divine Knowledge*, which he describes as " preparatory to a new Edition of the Works of Jacob Behmen [Boehme] ; and the right Use of them ". It is, however, more Boehme than Law, and is, therefore, outside the limits of our enquiry.

In writing about the flowering of English mysticism, and the guidance which various mystical writers can give in dealing with the dilemmas of to-day, it was essential to call attention to William Law. But to attempt an appreciation and explanation of his special contribution to mystical knowledge would be to trespass on a domain that Stephen Hobhouse has made his own. His book of *Selected Mystical Writings of William Law*, with his own comments and notes, is so complete and wholly admirable that no lover of Law would venture to do more than thankfully refer others to it. Nevertheless, it is allowable to point to two characteristic sentences from *The Spirit of Prayer* as signposts to the way of Law's mysticism :

" (1) The sun meets not the springing bud that stretches towards him with half that certainty as God, the source of all good, communicates Himself to the soul that longs to partake of Him.
" (2) A Christ not in us is a Christ not ours."

The mystical and ethical elements in religion found a worthy exponent in this man, whom W. R. Inge praises as " perhaps the foremost of our mystical divines ". It remains just to say a word about his outward life ; for his biography explains his attitude towards the third element in religion, institutionalism. He was born in 1686, ordained in 1711, and, on the accession of George I, became a Non-juror. This was one reason why he eventually lived a life of retirement, in his native village of King's Cliffe, where he tried to carry out the principles of conduct set forth in *A Serious Call*, including the duty of loyalty to institutional religion as he understood it. He numbered among his friends men of such different types as John Byrom the Nonjuror, Edward Gibbon the historian, and John Wesley ; though friendships were a fluctuating experience in the life of one so unswerving in principle and outspoken in intercourse as Law was. It is characteristic that he should have ventured to rebuke the redoubtable John Wesley in the memorable words, " You would have a philosophical religion, but there can be no such thing. Religion is the most plain, simple thing in the world ; it is only, We love Him because He first loved us ". Anyone who has read the nine volumes of Law's Collected Works would find it hard to discover in them that " religion is the most plain, simple thing in the world ".

Thomas Traherne (1636-1674) was a mystic of a very different type from the devotional à Kempis (though he knew *The Imitation*, and quoted from it), or the ethical-intellectual Law. Their only kinship consisted in their underlying mysticism. Traherne is one of those writers, like G. K. Chesterton, whose effervescence is so fascinating that many readers miss something of their true depth. He is classed, superficially, as a delightful optimist, full of the joy of living, rejoicing in the friendliness of nature, and the benevolence of God. There is nothing wrong in this view ; it is true as far as it goes : but it is grievously incomplete. If it were the whole truth, Traherne could scarcely be called a mystic ; whereas he was not only a mystic, but he contributed a fresh facet to the shining jewel of mysticism. His paradoxical insistence on the possessiveness of man and the yearning " want " of God, if rightly understood, exhibits a sound spiritual truth which is a reaction, justified though perhaps exaggerated, against the conception of the nothingness of man and the self-absorption of God, as taught by the disciples of Plotinus down to the present time. Traherne refused to believe that God is *uninterested* in what He has made ; or that the Creation is, in its true being, unworthy

of the Creator's love. Over and over again he insists on
the twin-truths of his philosophy :

" You must want like a God that you may be satisfied
like God. Were you not made in His Image ? He is
infinitely Glorious, because all his wants and supplies are
at the same time in his nature from Eternity. He had,
and from Eternity He was without all His Treasures.
From Eternity He needed them, and from Eternity He
enjoyed them. For all Eternity is at once in Him, both
the empty durations before the World was made, and the
full ones after. His wants are as lively as His enjoyments :
and always present with Him. For His life is perfect,
and He feels them both. His wants put a lustre upon
His enjoyments and make them infinite. His enjoyments
being infinite crown His wants, and make them beautiful
even to God Himself. His wants and enjoyments being
always present are delightful to each other, stable, immutable, perfective of each other, and delightful to Him.
Who being Eternal and Immutable, enjoyeth all His
wants and treasures together. His wants never afflict
Him, His treasures never disturb Him. His wants always
delight Him ; His treasures never cloy Him. The sense
of His wants is always as great, as if His treasures were
removed : and as lively upon Him. The sense of His
wants, as it enlargeth His life, so it infuseth a value, and
continual sweetness into the treasures He enjoyeth."

The answering note to this conception of Divine " want "
permeates all his writing, and may be found summed up in
another famous passage :

" You never enjoy the world aright, till the Sea itself
floweth in your veins, till you are clothed with the heavens,
and crowned with the stars : and perceive yourself to be
the sole heir of the whole world, and more than so,
because men are in it who are every one sole heirs as well
as you. Till you can sing and rejoice and delight in God,
as misers do in gold, and Kings in sceptres, you never
enjoy the world."

In spite of the beauty of these two conceptions, character-istic of Traherne, they might almost jar on the mystical sensitiveness of some readers, by a sort of excess of originality, were it not that he combined them with his experience of what sin means. His was no shallow optimism, the result of shutting the eyes to the exceeding sinfulness of sin, and its blasting consequences. He had a deep-rooted love for the Passion of the Saviour ; and he knew, by experience, some-thing of that dereliction which called forth the cry of the Crucified, " *My God, my God, why hast Thou forsaken me* ". He knew the incubus of the mystics' Dark Night of the Soul —" heart-ache kindled into love "—which is a sharing of the Passion :

> " O Thou Son of Righteousness, eclipsed on the Cross, overcast with sorrows, and crowned with the shadow of death, remove the veil of Thy flesh that I may see Thy glory. Those cheeks are shades, those limbs and members clouds, that hide the glory of Thy mind, Thy knowledge and Thy love from us. But were they removed those inward excellencies would remain invisible. As therefore we see Thy flesh with our fleshly eyes, and handle Thy wounds with our bodily senses, let us see Thy under-standing with our understandings, and read Thy love with our own. Let our souls have communion with Thy soul, and let the eye of our mind enter into Thine. Who art Thou who bleeding here causest the ground to tremble and the rocks to rend, and the graves to open ? Hath Thy death influence so high as the highest Heavens ? That the Sun also mourneth and is clothed in sables ? Is Thy spirit present in the temple, that the veil rendeth in twain at Thy passion ? O let me leave Kings' Courts to come unto Thee, I choose rather in a cave to serve Thee, than on a throne to despise Thee. O my Dying Gracious Lord, I perceive the virtue of Thy passion everywhere : Let it, I beseech Thee, enter into my Soul and rend my rocky, stony heart, and tear the veil of my flesh, that I may see into the Holy of Holies ! O darken the Sun of pride and vain-glory. Yea, let the sun itself

be dark in comparison of Thy love ! And open the grave of my flesh, that my soul may arise to praise Thee. Grant this for Thy mercy's sake. Amen ! " [8]

There is no shallow optimism about that prayer of Traherne's. He has been accused of religious emotionalism ; but religious emotionalism, if sincere and persistent, is that " perpetual aspiration towards God " which, as S. Augustin affirms, constitutes the true life of a Christian. No glib taunt about unworthy emotionalism can be flung at a mystic who could make the great appeal to the intellectual element in religion that Traherne made when he proclaimed that " to think well is to serve God in the interior court ".

The seventeenth century was rich in the unfolding of mysticism as the fourteenth century had been. Both were periods of outward turmoil and strife. When we think of the Civil War in England, and all that it must have meant to the lives of men and women in that seventeenth century, it seems almost incredible that Isaak Walton's *Compleat Angler* should have been produced in 1653, Sir Thomas Browne's *Religio Medici* in 1642, Robert Herrick's *Hesperides* in 1648, and that George Herbert should have written *The Temple* two years before Laud was made Archbishop, when party feeling was already tempestuous. In the thirty years between 1630 and 1660, some of the most restful books in the English language were written ; and, though Traherne's work, like that of another inspired mystic, Henry Vaughan, was probably not written till the close of this period, it carries on the same tradition, and gives little evidence of the stormy scenes of which, as a youth, he must have been witness.

I have included Traherne among prose writers rather than among poets, not by a presumptuous assumption of literary judgment, but because it seems to me that prose is the medium through which his thought finds its clearest and most natural expression. This reference to his poetry must be the excuse for what appears to be a digression from the particular subject of this chapter. It is not irrelevant, however, to our main purpose of illustrating from the mystics of the past something of the possibilities of mysticism in the present ; to pursue for a moment a by-path into which Traherne's poems lead us : *Is there some special psychic affinity between mystics ?* Does that affinity overpass the limitations of time and space ?

It is a rather amusing thought that if Traherne's poems had been written about the time when they were first published, in the early part of this century (instead of more than 200 years before), he would certainly have been accused of plagiarism, and even of slavish imitation. Critics would have confidently affirmed that he borrowed ideas and forms from Wordsworth, Walt Whitman, and Francis Thompson. It says much for the breadth of his genius that he appears to have close harmonies with such diverse writers.

It is natural that there should be a fundamental likeness between Thompson and Traherne due to the fact that both were mystics. There is, however, much more than a similarity of outlook. Any careful student of Traherne's poems will discover in them a likeness in idea and in the detail of working it out, passages that are reminiscent of those particular visions of Thompson, the pursuing love of God as described in *The Hound of Heaven*, and the nearness of Christ revealed in *In No Far Land*. The verbal inventiveness and flamboyance of both poets is striking, but less significant. The likeness of some of Traherne's poems to those of Walt Whitman is still more noticeable, and still more surprising. It is difficult to realise that such verses as these were written before America had a literature at all, and so, long before the days of Walt Whitman :

Thou, Lord, hast made thy servant a sociable creature,
    for which I praise thy name,
A lover of company, a delighter in equals ;
Replenish the inclinations which Thyself hath implanted,

And give me eyes
To see the beauty of that life and comfort
Wherewith those by their actions
    Inspire the nations.
Their Markets, Tillage, Courts of Judicature, Marriages,
    Feasts and Assemblies, Navys, Armies,
Priests and Sabbaths, Trades and Business, the voice of
    the Bridegroom, Musical Instruments, the light of
    Candles, and the grinding of Mills. . . .
They are my Factors, Substitutes, and Stewards ;
Second Selves, who by Trade and Business animate my
    wealth,
Which else would be dead and rust in my hands.

No wonder that B. Dobell, who first discovered Traherne's writings and published them, remarks, " Have we not here a very remarkable anticipation of the leading thought of Whitman's *Leaves of Grass* ? " He might have added, " Have we not here an astounding anticipation of the form in which Whitman clothed his thought and of his supposedly unique peculiarities ? "

It is, however, in the amazing likeness between Traherne and Wordsworth that there appears to be the most interesting opening for psychical research. To quote Dobell, once again : " Another poet with whom Traherne has some remarkable affinities is Wordsworth—not the Wordsworth of later life, when his poetic vein, if not exhausted, had at least grown thin and unproductive, but the Wordsworth of the magnificent ode *Intimations of Immortality, from Recollections of Early Childhood.* Let the reader once more peruse that poem, and note carefully the leading points in it. Then let him, bearing in mind the (apposite) extracts from Traherne's *Centuries of Meditations*, go carefully through the various poems in which the earlier poet celebrates the happiness of his infancy and childhood. When he has done this, let him ask himself if he would have believed that Wordsworth was unacquainted with Traherne's writings, supposing that they had been published before the later poet's time ?   I cannot think myself that it would have been easy in that case to think that the modern poet was entirely unindebted to the older one.   It is hardly too much to say that there is not a thought of any value in Wordsworth's Ode which is not to be found in substance in Traherne." It is, in truth, scarcely an exaggeration to say that a proportion of the poetry of both men was interchangeable.

Is there, as some reputable men of science have suggested, some atmosphere of locality that acts as a sort of sensitive photographic plate, recording impressions ?   This suggestion was made, primarily, to account for well-authenticated cases of apparition such as those referred to by Hardy in *Tess of the D'Ubervilles* : according to local superstitions, it is said that the D'Uberville coach passes over Wool bridge and draws up at the Manor on Christmas Eve, an event for which there is no lack of evidence.   But the suggestion might cover a more ethereal or spiritual category than that of visual appearances.   It is, at least, a very remarkable coincidence that Traherne lived at Credenhill Rectory, and *only a short walk away* was Brinsop Court, where Wordsworth frequently stayed with his relations the Hutchinsons.

This suggests long lanes of exploration into the relations between the psychical and the mystical, which, however, cannot be fully followed here.   Yet it does not do to leave entirely out of account the possibility that thought-transference from age to age, as well as from place to place, is a manifestation of a bigger synthesis of life than a merely " matter-of-fact " attitude of mind can reveal.   In broad outline the case for consideration might be set out in this way : a man might say that all religions alike seek for a reconciliation between the individual and the whole, which is regarded either as God or as the soul of the universe, and for some doctrine of their relations which shall not wholly extinguish one in the other.   He might add, like the author of the fourth Gospel, that the key to the problem is to be found in love ; endeavouring at the same time to give this doctrine, which in religion is purely mystical, a scientific basis by relating it to modern biology and carrying it forward into speculations which embrace not only the human future but the cosmic destiny. This man of " scientific " predisposition would find in the behaviour of the primitive germ cells the working of the principle which extends to the conscious love of human beings, and far beyond it to the whole process of nature in the world and the universe. In each and all he would see the soul of the universe energising to make itself conscious, and find self-expression. In this progression all the stages from the primitive cells through the animal to the human are linked together, and tend towards some far-off Divine event in which the individual shall be gathered up into the whole, and partake of the full consciousness of the whole, and yet retain its capacity to enjoy its share of the whole. The link is love, and it both informs and permeates the subconscious life, while at the same time it keeps the individual a conscious unit in the main stream of consciousness, which is independent of death. If this is so, it is conceivable that, at times, there should be an " inhibition of thought " (and an illumination of imagination) enabling you to become aware of your real self as pervading the life of other creatures and moving in bodies other than your so-called own.

This is an aspect of thought transference which, if accepted, leads on to the assertion that it does not much matter, once you have experienced this state, whether the one body remains or passes ; all is transcended by thought. This, we are told, is the language of the ascetic and the mystic ; or at any rate it is a doctrine attributed to them. It is necessary to admit, however, that for the daily routine of work in the world *it does very much matter* whether the one body remains or passes ; or we might at times be tempted to change existences as we change houses. Nevertheless, we need not for that reason eschew the testimony of the mystics hinting at this surviving unity, of which some prophets and religious teachers have assured us, and of which we have occasional glimpses in our own experience. They are for a large number of people the principal intimations of human immortality, and a light, however dim, on some of the deeper enigmas of life.

To return from speculation to fact, mystical writers acted and reacted on one another in the ordinary ways of human influence, and the recognised methods by which one man helps another ; partly by speech, partly by writing, partly by example, as well as in other ways. In this respect, the supernatural does not rule out the natural, nor the natural the supernatural. William Law, as has been said, derived much of his mysticism from Boehme. So did a very different man, Charles Kingsley. But they were neither of them " possessed " by him ; nor did they just reproduce Boehme, as a preacher often reproduces the latest book he has been reading. Each of them contributed his modicum of originality to the literature of mysticism. Each of them remained British ; and there was nothing British about Boehme. In other words, they did more than read ; they did more than learn and mark ; they inwardly digested Boehme. They were not moulded into his likeness, and for that very reason they were able to interpret him ; for an interpreter must always be, in part, a looker-on, preserving his own integrity of mind and acting as a link between two other minds.

It is in friendships, however, like the friendship between S. Teresa and S. John of the Cross, that the most fruitful reaction takes place. Perhaps it is in this fact that the propagandist strength of mysticism lies, for mystics are naturally friends with one another : they speak the same language, and accept the same code of values—the outward and inward means to harmony in human fellowship. The man who wants to understand mysticism, and become a mystic, must be the friend of all other mystics (to whom God is all-in-all), here and beyond.

If he can live in the same spiritual home, accepting the same habit of loyalty that is found in institutionalism, he will find it a valuable factor towards the happiness of *the fellowship of the mystery*.   At the same time he will escape that heretical bitterness which mars some of the writings of solitary mystics like Swedenborg or Irving.   This happiness of fellowship in a common loyalty was pregnant in the lives of Traherne and Law, and countless others.   The specula-tive genius of their master Boehme never transformed Law or Kingsley into anything other than English clergymen, though it helped to make them *inspired* English clergymen. Traherne, too, was a loyal son of the Church of England, a country parson of the Herbert tradition.   His great con-temporaries were as little tainted with heresy as he was : indeed, the seventeenth century was notable for its happy fellowship of loyalists.   The name of Nicholas Ferrar of Little Gidding springs to mind as one of the chief bonds in this most attractive brotherhood.   All alike gave their whole-hearted allegiance to the institutional religion of their time, finding in it a sure foundation and a safe starting-point for the exuberance of their devotional flights into the realm of mysticism.   They were not mystics *in spite* of being institutionalists, but *because* of being institutionalists.   In the *quietness and confidence* of assured tradition they found their *strength*.

CHAPTER VI

MYSTICISM IN POETRY

POETRY and mysticism go hand in hand. Dante, great poet and great mystic, is the supreme exemplar of this truth. Poetry and mysticism are the warp and the weft in the fabric of his three masterpieces. They supply both the substance and the colour, wedded in design. Not all poets, however, have the twin-inspiration of a Dante ; and of those who are both poets and mystics there are none who do not fall short of their great exemplar. Nor is all poetry of necessity mystical : drama in verse or history in verse may be little more than drama or history. In such a case, poetry is just an embellishment : it presents the theme in such a form as to give it grandeur and emotional appeal, and make it memorable. But verse as verse does little to reveal the meaning of the incidents portrayed. And there can be no mysticism in poetry unless it has the quality of revelation.

There is nothing essentially mystical about the poetry of Homer, or of Shakespeare in his plays. Both are poets of an inspired and magnificent humanism ; their references to the Divine are, at root, incidental. It is in lyrical and elegiacal poetry that mysticism is chiefly to be found. It might even be maintained that there is no first-grade lyrical or elegiacal poetry which is not mystical. There are, indeed, lyrical poems, not obviously mystical, which live by sheer beauty of words and cadence ; but their appeal and their power are subject to the fleeting fashions of literary taste : they lack universality. Men look for more than beauty in the highest poetry. Nothing is more certain than that most lovers of poetry expect to find in the reading of the poets a spiritual illumination about the life of nature, and the life of man ; especially as they are related to the harmony of supreme being, which most men call " God ". In a word, they expect—and have a right to expect—*revelation*.

As a means to the better understanding of mysticism in poetry, it is permissible to dwell on three aspects—" Nature-mysticism ", " Humanity-mysticism ", " Church-mysticism", —always remembering, however, that the supreme mysticism is that which gives direct illumination to man of the nature and being of God. To this transcendent end poetry may contribute ; but its contribution, like all other human means to a Divine end, is at most an enhancement of receptivity. " God "-mysticism is not man's creation ; it is God's gift, the revelation of His bounty.

Four-fifths of the mysticism in poetry of the last two hundred years is nature-mysticism. It speaks of the sacramental nature of the universe in its varied manifestations, proclaiming the inward and spiritual in the outward and visible :

> All are but parts of one stupendous whole,
> Whose body nature is, and God the soul.

This aspect of mysticism is kaleidoscopic, " offering an endless variety of beautiful colours and forms ". It is impossible to give any complete account of it. In English poetry it finds its best-known expression in Wordsworth. He is the high priest who initiates the nature-loving Englishman into the mysteries of nature's meaning. At his best, he helps to meet not only the vague desire to understand the emotion which the beauty of nature stirs in human hearts, but also that craving for spiritual things which can only be satisfied by a higher order of harmony than nature can offer :

> The universal instinct of repose ;
> The longing for confirmed tranquility,
> Inward and outward ; humble yet sublime :
> The life where hope and memory are as one ;
> Earth quiet and unchanged ; the human soul
> Consistent in self-rule ; and heaven revealed
> To meditation, in that quietness !

Wordsworth exhibits both the strength and the weakness of this aspect of mysticism. His life, blameless in respectability during his later years, was not entirely " consistent in self-rule " ; partly because self-rule never can be consistent, and partly because there can be no genuine self-rule apart from the acceptance of a wider loyalty and of a standard of values based on an external authority having the right to impose that standard. In the galaxy of poets, Wordsworth was a bright planet revolving smoothly on his own axis, but erratic in his revolving round the sun. As a poet, he nobly succeeded ; as a man, he was more fallible. There is truth, sad though it be, in the summing up of his nature by a modern critic, " Perverse as his whole character is shown, however unwittingly, in Dorothy's journal to be : with his moods, his illnesses, his fretful and domineering and ungrateful ways, his indolence, and his monumental seriousness about himself."

There seems to be in the poets of nature-mysticism an inherent tendency towards self-centredness. They are not completely taken out of themselves, because they cannot forget themselves. Their failure to reach, through the contemplation of nature, to the highest peaks of mysticism is inevitable ; for creaturely things can never permanently lift the creature Man out of his creatureliness ; only the Divine can do that. There is, therefore, an incompleteness about nature-mysticism caused partly by its vagueness, and partly by its dependence on the fluctuating authority of human insight. It is a revelation which is mainly a self-revelation ; a " projection " devoid of external sanction ; the reaction of a subject to an object when the subject is greater than the object, for the human spirit is always greater than the material universe. So it comes about that both the matter and its expression are vague. The man who proclaims that he feels " at one with the throbbing heart of Mother Earth " does not really know what he means : just as the man who despises the disciplined loyalty of united worship and

" communes with God in the green fields and under the
blue sky " is usually humbugging himself, and others,
through ignoring the meaning of " communing " and of
" God ", the key-notes of his boast.   There is no escaping
the fact that consciousness of his place in a Divine Society
is an essential element in the working out of man's highest
destiny.   It is the mystic whose feet are firmly planted on
the rock of institutionalism who is most capable of expound-
ing, with balance and power, the glorious truths—or half-
truths—of nature-mysticism.

Humanity-mysticism, the sense of one-ness with all
fellow-men, is an experience essential to the true understanding of life.   *We are members one of another*.   It lies at the
root of that spirit of social service which is one of the glories
of our time.   It has inspired some of the greatest poets.
Walt Whitman's poetry exhibits it in notable form.   Many
people, however, feel that it is a perverted form, in that it is
carried too far, to the exclusion of higher things.   They
would agree that Aldous Huxley is justified in his penetrating
ruthlessness when he refers to " the sublimated sexual
mysticism of Whitman ".   There is much in modern literature to prove or exemplify how necessary is the outspoken-
ness of this criticism.   None the less, humanity-mysticism is
a very valuable aspect of the whole.   In a form healthier
than Whitman's it is found in much of Masefield's poetry.
His homeliness commends it ; and his linking of it with
nature-mysticism expands it, and makes it more satisfying.
In *The Everlasting Mercy*, his hero is in very truth one of the
people and one with the people ; he is an animal having
mystical affinities with his fellow animals :

> The men who don't know to the root
> The joy of being swift of foot,
> Have never known divine and fresh
> The glory of the gift of flesh,
> Nor felt the feet exult, nor gone
> Along a dim road, on and on,

Knowing again the bursting glows,
The mating hare in April knows,
Who tingles to the pads with mirth
At being the swiftest thing on earth.

A few lines further on, he rises to the level of the higher mysticism in a revealing passage of homely beauty :

And he who gives a child a treat
Makes joy-bells ring in Heaven's street,
And he who gives a child a home
Builds palaces in Kingdom come,
And she who gives a baby birth
Brings Saviour Christ again to Earth,
For life is joy, and mind is fruit,
And body 's precious earth and root.[9]

It is the quality of spiritual vision which makes the under-current of Masefield's poetry a nobler philosophy than that of most of his fellow-poets of the humanity-mysticism school. He prepares the way for a step higher—to the religious mysticism of Browning, who, in *An Epistle* [of Karshish] and in other poems, by implication, sets the seal of divinity upon humanity, and makes humanity-mysticism into God-mysticism by proclaiming the universal message of the Incarnation, and its all-embracing consequences offering the Divine gift of fellowship to men.

Church-mysticism, the one-ing of the soul with its Mother is no mere perversion of something higher—the one-ing of the soul with its Father.   It may be and must be a means to an end ; but it is so closely linked with the end that it is scarcely distinguishable from it.   I think it was S. Chrysostom who said, " you cannot have God for your father unless you have the Church for your mother ".   It is a saying easily misunderstood, but true in the sense that he spoke it.   So church-mysticism is true, though incom-plete.   If it emphasises one side of the truth to the detriment of other sides, it becomes a snare, but there is no false emphasis *inherent* in it. The accusation that the Church becomes substituted for God as the alpha and omega of a man's religion is sometimes true : *corruptio optimi pessima.* It is some justification for the popular suspicion of institutional religion. But, to turn to the witness of poetry in mysticism, it is an accusation which cannot be brought against the two poets whom we are to consider as heralds in this aspect of mysticism.

Francis Thompson and Coventry Patmore were both members of the Church of Rome ; Thompson by upbringing, Patmore by conversion. They sympathised, therefore, with the hierarchical outlook. But, in Thompson's case at any rate, it did not warp their spiritual judgment ; and he was infinitely the greater of the two. Both as a poet and as a mystic he overshadowed the friend whom he reverenced. V. Sackville-West, in her study of two notable Continental mystics, calls S. Theresa of Avila " the Eagle ", and S. Theresa of Lisieux " the Dove ". The eagle is said to be able to gaze on the sun ; the dove assuredly cannot. That was true of S. Theresa the Eagle and S. Theresa the Dove. It was equally true of Thompson and Patmore. One was an inspired mystic, the other, a mystical devotee. It is because of his limitations that Patmore is, in some respects, a better example of church-mysticism than Thompson is. The greater poet, that is to say, is not the best example of one approach, because he soars above any single aspect of mysticism. His ecclesiastical insight and imagination are harnessed to a super-ecclesiastical purpose, as he draws from the ceremonial of the Church images to clothe his mystical thought ; at the same time sinking his identity in the embrace of his divinely-ordained Mother.

No one, in all English literature, has worked out this line of mystical approach with such an uplifting splendour as Thompson has done it, as, for example, in his *Orient Ode :*

Lo, in the sanctuaried East,
Day, a dedicated priest
In all his robes pontifical exprest,
Lifteth slowly, lifteth sweetly,
From out its Orient tabernacle drawn,
Yon orbèd sacrament confest
Which sprinkles benediction through the dawn ;
And when the grave procession's ceased,
The earth with due illustrious rite
Blessed,—ere the frail fingers featly
Of twilight, violet-cassocked acolyte,
His sacerdotal stoles unvest—
Sets, for high close of the mysterious feast,
The sun in august exposition meetly
Within the flaming monstrance of the West.[10]

Patmore, the dove, never wrote anything comparable with
that.   His published verse " falls sharply into two divisions,
of which the first might be called the angelico-domestic, and
the second, the incognito-erotic ".   In the first division he
sings of wedded love as the sacrament of the love between
the soul and God, rising to heights of beautiful symbolism.
But he was talented rather than inspired, a type rather than
a model.   None the less, he earns our gratitude by bearing
his unexpected witness that " mysticism is the most complete
and definite kind of spiritual apprehension of which man is
capable ".

Both these mystics wrote prose not unworthy to be set
beside their verse.   Some of the most trustworthy critics of
literature judge Thompson's *Essay on Shelley* to be one of the
finest pieces of prose in the English language.   He paints
his word-picture with bold and unerring strokes of the brush.
Patmore, on the other hand, excels in epigram, stippling in
the dainty details of wisdom in miniature.   In these little
sayings he discloses, better than in his longer poems, the
sincerity of his mysticism.   Here are examples :

" So give me to possess this mystery that I shall not desire to understand it.

" When first you unite yourself by charity to the whole human race, then shall you perceive indeed that Christ died for you."

(This might be confirmed and exemplified in the words of a very different type of mystic, George Macdonald, " To find God in others is better than to grow solely in the discovery of Him in ourselves, if indeed the latter were possible.")   Finally, Patmore bears the mystic's witness to the value of institutional religion in declaring :

" The Catholic Church alone teaches as matters of faith those things which the thoroughly sincere person of any sect discovers, more or less obscurely, for himself, but does not believe for want of external sanction."

The consideration of these three aspects of mysticism— nature-mysticism, humanity-mysticism, and church-mysticism—can be supplemented by another cross-section of the subject.   There is a useful distinction to be drawn between what may be called the poetry of the transcendent, and the poetry of the immanent.   Some mystical poets see more clearly the descending angels on Jacob's ladder ; others, the ascending.   There are, that is to say, poets who soar to Heaven, and bring down to earth-bound mortals something of what they have contemplated.   There are others who find the Creator in His creation, the spiritual in the material. To them, God is not only the transcendental Creator, He is also the Sustainer of the universe :

> Lord, purge our eyes to see
> Within the seed a tree,
> Within the glowing egg a bird,
> Within the shroud a butterfly.
>
> Till taught by such, we see
> Beyond all creatures Thee,
> And hearken to Thy tender word,
> And hear it, " Fear not : it is I ".

It is this conception which is the key-note of much the larger output of mystical verse. In fact, it is the poetry of immanence that is popularly accepted as being mystical.

There is no less mysticism, however, in the poetry of transcendence. It. is, of course, the very essence and root of Dante's poetry that he reveals a vision of spiritual realities, as it were from above. He stands alone and unapproachable in the majesty of his revelation. Yet there are many other lesser lights who may be classed as poets of the transcendent rather than poets of the immanent. Shelley, for instance, is a poet of vision rather than of interpretation. Warped he may have been, but he was undoubtedly a transcendentalist. Like Keats, he could say :

> I was taught in Paradise
> To ease my breast of melodies.

There is no less mysticism in looking to earth from Heaven than in looking to Heaven from earth. To see the earth as God sees it, and to proclaim that vision, however imperfectly, is one of the triumphs of mystical poetry.

On the other hand, the poetry of immanence, the interpretation of the seen in terms of the unseen, makes the wider appeal. This is what poetry means for most of us. It is the enlightenment to which the human soul most readily reacts, unless it is bogged in sensuality and materialism. William Blake, seeing " a World in a grain of sand ", in poem after poem, illustrates this truth ; a truth that inebriates him with a sense of the omnipresence of the Divine. He gives expression, as do countless other poets, to the aspiration inherent in the spirit of man, the cry of " Excelsior " :

> I give you the end of a golden string :
> Only wind it into a ball,
> It will lead you in at Heaven's gate,
> Built in Jerusalem's wall.

In a different fashion, but no less persistently, Francis
Thompson proclaims the ladder " betwixt Heaven and
Charing Cross ". All true lyrical poets alike, whether from
the angle of spiritual transcendence or of spiritual immanence,
give us, each in his way, that vision of values which is
mysticism. However they view the angels of the ladder,
all alike have Beth-el, the house of God, as their abiding
place.

Mystical poetry is, for the most part, religious poetry.
For the most part, too, its Muse is cradled in institutionalism.
Even in a time of civil and religious disintegration, like the
seventeenth century in England, the true poets held fast to
their anchorage of faith. There was no vague wildness of
unorthodoxy about Traherne, Herbert, Quarles, Crashaw,
Herrick, Vaughan, and the other stars in the crowded
firmament of seventeenth-century mystical poetry. Nor
were these shining lights in any way exotic. They fitted
in to their time and their surroundings ; as H. J. Massingham
points out in a wisely balanced estimate of their value as
spiritual interpreters of their time and their place :

" The flaming felicity of Traherne, so different from
the enchanting folk-rusticity and joyous worldliness of
Parson Herrick, is a new idea both in English poetry and
ecclesiastical history. In thought, what a world away
indeed was the Rector of Dean Prior from the Rector of
Credenhill, both country parsons, both lovers and celeb-
rants of earth, both living in the seventeenth century !
Herrick's nature was almost wholly pre-Christian ; Traherne equally accepting her loveliness and in love with it,
saw the green world as the very body of God. Still more
so Vaughan, who, calling himself 'The Silurist' and 'Olor
Iscanus ', is thus one of the very earliest of our regional
ruralists. Except in S. Francis and the early saints, this
conception of nature is not to be found in Catholicism.
It is a novelty added on to the mediæval tradition, and its
due importance in our study of the continuity of the
English tradition will be more fully realised when we come

to Hawker and Barnes. Therefore, this triple achievement of Herbert, Vaughan and Traherne, if more fragmentary and defective than that of Wordsworth and
Coleridge in the Lyrical Ballads, takes momentous place
in the history of rural Anglicanism. . . . Yet this trio,
sharing this mystical experience in common, is entirely
different in poetic expression. Herbert, whom Vaughan
regarded as his master, shows a wonderful dramatic
power in his endings, while Vaughan's unearthly inspiration so often goes into sunset before his poem is finished.
Herbert loved analogies and similies taken from village
lore and the little familiar things of village life. He made
a collection of local proverbial sayings and in Steps to
the Temple laid down self-imposed precepts of a pastor's
spiritual courtesies and sympathies towards his flock.
Vaughan, though often extremely simple, is at the same
time starry and elemental in his choice of natural symbols.
Yet these poets all belong to one school, the school of
Donne, which, often recondite, tasteless and compromised
by what Addison called ' false wit ', yet has seen further
into the ultimate mysteries of life and nature than any
modern." [11]

These " regional ruralists " are embedded in the fabric
of English mysticism, children of no alien soil. Their
poetry blossomed as the natural outcome of their lives.
They wrote religious poetry because they were religious men.
The effort made by nineteenth-century critics to separate
the religion of poets like Vaughan from their mysticism
(and their poetry) was simply dishonest. Not to consider
Vaughan as a man of his time, declares that trustworthy
writer Helen White, is unfair. It is to view him, as many
nineteenth-century critics did, as a less great Wordsworth or
as a vague nature-lover who forfeited his animistic birth-
right for a mess of seventeenth-century orthodoxy. Not to
remember that the source of all his religious ideas and
tastes lay in the Church to which he belonged is to miss the
intellectual back-bone of his work, and to ask more of the

emotional and imaginative elements than we have any right to ask. We may go further, and say that Vaughan's religious genius raised him from being an excellent but second-rate minor poet, an imitator of Donne and Crashaw and Herbert, into a poet worthy to rank with the greatest of them.

In one respect he is unrivalled among the mystical writers of his time. He explores, with a talented originality, a by-path of nature-mysticism, and reveals what others have felt and been unable to express, " the sense of a veil between the soul of man and the world which he looks upon ". The theological derivation of this sad state (and the only satisfying explanation of it) is to be found in the doctrine of the Fall. In Eden, man is one with all life ; nature, including human nature, is one vast harmony. But the dissonance of sin has spoiled that perfection. It is this sense of something missing, this dislocation, this yearning after a lost perfection which colours the poetry of many nature-mystics with a very lovely wistfulness, and which finds its clearest expression in Vaughan.

These glimpses of a great literature, and the thought that underlies it, so fleeting and fragmentary, are in themselves as unsatisfying as the appetiser before a feast. It seems almost a mockery to lift just a tiny corner of the curtain, when there is so much to be seen behind it. None the less, if it leads on to an effort to see more, it is not without value towards the understanding of our main contention, that there is no inherent antagonism between the free spirit of mysticism and the disciplined spirit of brotherhood in religion. The best crop of mysticism grows in the well-cultivated communal field of theology. It is not just a harvest of beautiful weeds, sown by the wind of caprice.

MYSTICISM AND INSTITUTIONALISM

THIS is the pivotal chapter of my book. On it all the others hinge. What has gone before is neither an attempt to write a treatise on mysticism, nor an excursion into literary criticism. It is a preparation, more or less provocative, for finding an answer to a question. Like the searchlights which try to focus on a definite objective in order that the guns may do their work, the foregoing chapters play on the objective from many different angles. They are just means to an end, having no completeness in themselves, but hoping to produce the revealing " cone " of light. Now the time has come to consider the end, and to try to find an answer to the question : Has mysticism a vital part to play in the religion, and consequently in the life, of the present generation ? This involves several subsidiary questions. It is necessary, for instance, to discover whether there is any special need of reinforcement in religion as it is popularly presented ; and, if so, how the reinforcement is to be absorbed into the greater whole, and how it is to be used to best advantage so as to make its power felt.

The first of these subsidiary questions will be answered without hesitation, by religious and irreligious alike : if the Christian religion is to prevail, and be what it is meant to be in the world, it certainly needs reinforcement and re-newed life. The note of power and confident aggression is lacking. Faithfulness rather than zeal is the mark of modern orthodoxy. Boredom is the mark of modern unorthodoxy. This boredom, however, is not boredom with religion as such, but with religion as the ordinary outsider sees it. Press and radio bear witness to an intense interest in religion ; but the fellowship of worshipping Christians shows no signs of increase ; rather, there is a falling-away from all corporate and organised religious life.

For this state of affairs there is a steady flood of suggested palliatives. Never have the leaders of the Church shown a keener desire for evangelism, and all that evangelism stands for. The results, unfortunately, are pitifully far from being commensurate with their efforts. They strive to meet a need which does not exist, instead of tackling the infinitely harder task of creating a need. It is for them to enter into the spirit of their Master's heart-broken reproach, *Ye will not come to me, that ye might have life.* The will-to-life is absent because the meaning of life is misunderstood ; that is to say, men think of " eternal life " as existence infinitely prolonged. They have no conception of the truth that what Christianity has to offer is not length of existence but *fullness* of life, with *continuity* here and beyond. *Thou shalt show me the path of life ; in thy presence is the fullness of joy : and at thy right hand there is pleasure for evermore.* It is this sense of what life really means that is lacking. " Immortality " has no savour ; it seems to be wrapped up in a disguise of theological technicalities. The newly-coined word " immortability ", full of possibilities, may prove to be the pioneer of a new popular outlook on the future : men are not uninterested in being shown what they are capable of becoming.

Those words of Jesus—*Ye will not come unto me*—wrung from Him by grief that those whom He came to save made no response, are words of encouragement for us ; because they bear witness that He himself was faced by the very difficulty, absence of spiritual hunger, that His followers are inclined to think of as a difficulty peculiar to the twentieth century. He knew it ; and He sympathises with those who have to face it in its modern form. It was revealed to the mystics (and this is one of their most characteristic contributions to the message of the Church) that there is one infallible means of creating the sense of need, so that men will come to Jesus that they may have life. The need is created, not by preaching, not even by examples of well-doing, but by suffering : *I, if I be lifted up, will draw all men unto me.* The appeal of the Cross, if faithfully presented by men and women who are bearing the Cross, is irresistible. It is the mark of the wounds which makes men exclaim, with Thomas, *My Lord and my God.* So often, unfortunately, the various responses forget the power which evoked them, and tend to become robots of philanthrophy. No greater work is being done in the world to-day than the ministry of the British Red Cross. If the Cross in the title were ever to lose its meaning, it is absolutely certain that the work, founded on self-sacrifice, would wilt for lack of inspiration. It is true of the British Red Cross, and of numberless other organisa- tions for the welfare and healing of mankind, that they need to be recalled, from time to time, to a recognition of their origin in Christian teaching. Mysticism helps to fulfil this duty ; for it relates all sympathy with suffering to its true source on Calvary.

Not forgetting these deeper aspects of the matter, we go on to consider what are the commonest criticisms of " religion " to-day, why it is that institutionalism is the main object of attack, and whether it is true wisdom to reduce institutionalism to a minimum, or whether the best hope for the future does not lie in the infusion of a new spirit, the spirit of first-hand religion, into the forms and activities of organised Christianity.

It would be easy to write at length about the modern spirit of lawlessness, the resentment against any sort of compulsion, the contempt for authority, and the claim to unhindered self-expression. It has been done a hundred times, without any noticeable result. It is more profitable, I think, to examine the particular ways in which authority is flouted, and tradition defied. Why do people, otherwise sensible and well-meaning, keep on repeating the parrot-cry that they have no use for institutional religion? There must be some ground for their complaint; and it is worth while to examine it. People, and especially young people, say that religion is stuffy, and religious people are stuffy. They mean what they say, and they are far from wrong. Some vicars are inordinately prim; and some vicars' wives do wear impossible hats. Some churchwardens are indeed portentous. The weekly meeting of the Band of Hope lacks thrill. A lantern lecture with outworn slides is not up to the standard of the films at the nearest picture house. What these critics of institutionalism find, or do not find, in the public worship of the Church will be discussed later. Are they to be blamed for judging what they cannot see by what they cannot help seeing?

They are, of course, using the word "religion" in a very restricted sense, talking about a perversion of the real thing; but, unfortunately, it is a perversion that is obtruded upon their notice. Very often the bitterness of their criticism results from an unconscious resentment against what they feel is a sham. For at heart most of them are gropingly religious. It is, in truth, unreality in religion that they are condemning; not that they think the vicar a humbug, but that they cannot understand how a minister of the heroic Christ can be such a ninny. In any case, their condemnation of paltriness and their dissatisfaction with the unreality of mere window-dressing are all to the good, provided only that they go on to seek reality. It is sad that the contribution which they might make is often missing; because they stop short at criticism, and relapse into mental and spiritual lethargy. There are shirkers, interpreting the question, " Why doesn't the Church do something? " as meaning, " Why don't you do something? " instead of giving it the true interpretation, " Why don't I do something? " Nevertheless, in some cases, there is no doubt that if their criticism is received in a welcoming spirit, it grows more constructive. It is not infrequently the fault

of " religious " people that well-intentioned critics are
" put off " by being snubbed. In other cases, the critics
are critics only. They refuse to enter upon the quest for
reality, because they have a strong suspicion as to where
it will lead them. They have not the courage to face the
consequences, and to pay the price : *He went away grieved :
for he had great possessions.*

It is a factor in the situation to-day, which cannot be
ignored, that the call to sacrifice implies a bigger loss of
material advantages than in past ages. Life has been made
so easy ; men have such " great possessions " of comfort,
and security, and recreation that the call to seek, first, the
Kingdom of God and His righteousness falls on deaf ears.
" Why go to church on Sundays, when one can have a run
into the country by car, and a cheery lunch with friends at
some road-house ? "—that is how it strikes many young
people. Nor must it be taken for granted that it is only
selfish enjoyment that attracts them. Some of them do lead
strenuous lives, and need relaxation. There are many,
also, who find in secular learning—in books, in debating-
societies, on the radio, and in intercourse with like-minded
companions—a satisfaction of their mental aspirations,
whch anæsthetises any higher instinct of the spirit. Secular
learning, secular art, material comfort and prosperity seem
within the grasp of almost all. It is supposed to be only the
failures in life who turn to anything else. In which case,
religion can only be looked upon as a refuge for the destitute.
No wonder it is stuffy ! The vicious circle revolves ;
" religion " grows stuffy for want of help from those who
withdraw from it because it is stuffy.

It would be a mistake, however, to take a gloomy view
of the whole outlook. The experiencing of dissatisfaction
implies a belief in the possibility of satisfaction. There
must be a positive escape from the negative attitude. Diag-
nose the evil, and you are on the road to the good. The
diagnosis is being made ; the causes of the dissatisfaction

are being brought to light. There is a fuller atmosphere of sympathy, in which critics can breathe the health-bringing breeze of constructiveness. The evidence for this is found in many directions : there is, for example, the remarkable success of the " Padre's Hour " in the Services, and of informal " Brains-trusts " promoted by Toc H and other movements in which youth predominates. Frank discussion is the solvent of most difficulties : and, though the way may be long, a sign-post is being erected which points to Satisfaction.

In the mean time, courage is required to carry on ; a courage like that which sustained John the Baptist as he proclaimed the coming of the Conqueror. " The clergy of the Church of England are purveyors of an article that nobody wants." The truth of this remark is unquestionable. Every honest and intelligent clergyman knows it. It worries him by day and keeps him awake at night. It undermines his courage and breaks his heart. The better pastor he is, the more it is brought home to him, for the true pastor does not spend all his time in the fold with the faithful few. He goes out to discover not only the lost sheep, but also the members of the flock who have no use for the fold. It is little wonder, then, that some clergymen have an apologetic air, like the poor service men, after the last war, who went about trying to sell unwanted vacuum-cleaners. It requires an immense courage, and a deep-rooted faith in the Good Shepherd, to persevere year in year out in a service which meets with so little response : *O Jerusalem, Jerusalem . . . how often would I have gathered thy children together, even as a hen gathereth her chickens under her wings, and ye would not.*

The task is seen to be less hopeless than appears at first sight if we realise that it is an exaggeration to talk of *creating* a sense of need. Strictly speaking, only God can create. The task of the Christian minister is to awaken or reawaken the dormant religion, which is the heritage of man as man.

Faced by what appears to be a stalemate in the religious life of the nation, he has got to discover some way in which the war of attrition may be developed into a war of movement. This is not the place to consider in any detail the many schemes by which, in all earnestness, Christian leaders are setting themselves to deal with the stalemate.   In fact, it is scarcely worth while to consider the more popular of them, for those are, by their very nature, doomed to failure.   A scheme for awakening a sense of need by promising to purvey a more showy article—a brightly painted vacuum-cleaner which does not clean, or a Christianity without the Cross—is dishonest.   The preacher who tries to make Christianity an attractive and easy method of life, and commend it to his hearers as a labour-saving device, is more than a fool, he is a traitor.   Another futile scheme for " popularising religion " is by exploiting new methods of salesmanship, offering a bonus on purchases by tacking on promises of social amelioration to the stern message of *righteousness, temperance, and judgment to come*.   Mysticism, ever realistic, rejects palliatives and tries to get to the root of the evil, seeking a cure not merely an appeasement.

It must be remembered that the spiritual tragedy of to-day, religious sleeping-sickness, is a disease of a sophisticated populace in an artificial civilisation.   The disease is so overlaid with symptoms that it is difficult to trace where it really has its roots.   But the simple realism of mysticism pounces on those two symptoms of sophistication and artificiality, and diagnoses the disease as pride and self-sufficiency.   The mystics know the remedy ; because they have themselves tried it, and proved its worth : *Except ye be converted and become as little children, ye shall not enter into the kingdom of heaven.*

The contrast between the sleeping-sickness of civilisation and the eager, child-like sense of need exhibited by some of the primitive races is a striking contrast.   Nowhere has it been more clearly illustrated than in New Guinea during the present war. The natives, who were head-hunters and cannibals two generations ago, are now many of them Christians. Their religion is marked by the innate mysticism of child-like minds ; it loves symbolism, and finds the evidence of divinity in homely things. Moreover, it is intensely practical ; their faith issues in works. There has never been a nobler exhibition of Christ-like tenderness and self-sacrifice than is the work of the New Guinea natives as stretcher-bearers, guides, nurses, and porters in their willing co-operation with the forces of the Allies. To some of the soldiers of " civilisation " it has been a revelation of what religion really means. One of them, a hard-bitten Australian, voiced the feelings of many besides himself when he declared, " After seeing the way these chaps were ready to sacrifice themselves for us, I have come to think that Christ must have been a black man ".

Religion permeates the whole life of the Christian natives of New Guinea, and makes heroes of them when the call to heroism comes. It is meant to permeate the whole life of every child of God. In a similar way, the mystical element is meant to permeate the whole of religion ; not to the exclusion of the other elements, but for their enrichment. Having stated these convictions in general terms, it now remains to go on to consider one application of them. Mysticism *in worship* is the crux of the whole matter. If we can reach right conclusions with regard to that, the entire subject of the value of mysticism, and its relationship with institutionalism, will be brought to a focus of understanding.

Begin by facing facts. Christian public-worship, in Europe, is not exercising the compelling power of attraction that it should. It has little of that converting influence of which S. Paul wrote to the congregation at Corinth : *If . . . there come in one that believeth not, or one unlearned, he is convinced of all, he is judged of all ; And thus are the secrets of his heart made manifest ; and so falling down on his face he will worship God, and report that God is in you of a truth.* In face of public worship as we know it, such a passage seems like mockery. An infidel stranger dropping in to Matins in a conventional English church is not so overcome by the atmosphere of devotion that he falls down on his face and worships God. Fortunately, Matins is ceasing to be the norm, and there is more hope of such a stranger being able to *report that God is in you of a truth.* This does not mean that a change from Matins to the Eucharist is a piece of infallible magic, compelling response. It is the love permeating the worship, love of God and love of neighbour, which is the converting force.

In facing facts about present-day worship it is right to produce evidence, in addition to recording personal impressions. Here is evidence from three very different sources :

(1) **Karl Barth**, after describing (in *The Word of God and the Word of Man*) with ruthless penetration, the contrast between what is *expected* and what is experienced in Lutheran Sunday-morning worship, sums up :

" It is miraculous enough that there are still so-called congregations and parishes. It would perhaps be better for us if there were none, in order that we might at least perceive that the hour had struck. At any rate we should not depend upon the patience of God, which meets us frequently in the patience, not to say the drowsiness of our audience, to save us from the penitence which is the first need of our generation." [12]

(2) **Hugh Shearman**, in his book, *The Bishop's Confession*, makes the hero, who is a clergyman of the Church of Ireland, say :

" I became increasingly sceptical and dissatisfied about my position and the position of the Church. There seemed to be a growing, unbridgeable gap between Christian teaching and institutions and real life. Every now and again a missioner used to come round the coast and set up his tent and convert some of my parishioners to his hell-fire doctrines. These converted people either joined some obscure, smug little sect or else lapsed altogether. The second generation in a converted family generally went to church nowhere and had no religion. I became more and more convinced that the institutional side of the Church was necessary, but I felt more and more that it was not being used to any purpose, that it was not advancing in any way but was very slowly losing ground." [13]

(3) The picture founded on the facts we are facing is, on the whole, a dark and gloomy one. The two foregoing witnesses record failure. They are conscious of it, and dumbfounded by it. They look around for a remedy. Do they look up ? One suspects that they have still to be convinced that *Rationalism is not enough.* For they say nothing of any attempt to attract or hold congregations by an ordering of worship in the *beauty* of holiness and of brotherliness. There is a dawning of hope in the picture as drawn by Gabriel Hebert :

" That the Church, being such as she is, should inspire a certain repulsion, is intelligible enough. But she also exercises an attraction ; and here I feel sure that it is not least the sacred actions and words of Christian worship that make to very many a deep appeal, and one that is not only or even chiefly æsthetic : that even when sermons are tiresome and hymns banal, the drama of the eucharistic rite and the words of the Prayer Book speak to them of a real relation of man to the Eternal, and inspire a hope that amid the disintegration of modern life, the confusion of belief, and the falling in ruins of the towers of Babel that human idealism tries to build, they may yet come to find that this sacred symbolism is an expression of reality, of the things which cannot be shaken, of the City which hath foundations, whose builder and maker is God.

" I write as an Anglican." [14]

Observation convinces me that the third of my quotations is nearest to the truth at the present time. Christian worshippers are, I feel sure, turning the corner from conventionality and self-centredness to—at least—experiment. None the less, the generality of congregations lag fifty years behind the times ; so that it is still necessary, in trying to suggest ways in which institutional religion and worship may be imbued with the mystical spirit, to consider services which in their present position in the Church's scheme of worship are definitely out-of-place. Fortunately this dislocation of public worship, as evidenced in the substitution of Matins for the Lord's Service, on the Lord's Day, is gradually being remedied. On the other hand, there remain thousands of English churchmen who look upon Matins as their normal act of public worship. At the same time, there are thousands of occasional attendants at public worship who find in Matins (and to a less extent in Evensong) a good deal to criticise. Their criticisms are well-known—that much of the language is archaic ; that some of the Psalms are palpably immoral ; that many of the appointed Lessons are dull and boring, and without any message for our times ; that the expressions of penitence and of adoration are exaggerated and unreal.

These criticisms are, on their face-value, true. In this matter of worship, those who stick to the paths of early nineteenth-century conventionality are in danger of laying on men's shoulders *heavy burdens and grievous to be borne.* Matins is one of them, when it is allowed to usurp the foremost place in the worship of a parish ; and so long as its rendering is marked by a formality of correctness rather than by an attempt to make it intelligible. It is no use to resent the inevitable ; until the heavy burdens of misplaced services are removed, the wise and the truly Christian course is not to rebel against them, but to ease them, for ourselves and others, as best we may. This, again, is one of the contributions that mysticism can make towards a more satisfying wholeness of religion : it may inspire even a perverted institutionalism with the spirit of devotion and reality.

The mystics find in the Psalms a treasure-house of devotion. For themselves, they are able to sublimate the querulous complainings of a Jewish writer, or his blood-thirsty longings for vengeance on his visible foes, into an epic of the soul. They know that a Christian's foes are not so much without as within : he finds " Og the king of Bashan ", with all his surliness, at work in his own soul. Only God can deliver him from that tyranny. Moreover, the purple patches of prayer for vengeance and other aspirations out of harmony with the higher code of the New Testament are very few. The greater part of the Paslms can be recited without any misgiving ; and all can, if the Holy Spirit is at work in the heart of the worshipper. It is, incidentally, interesting to trace His work in the " mistakes " made by our English translators of these Hebrew hymns. How much more uplifting it is to sing " Worship the Lord in the beauty of holiness " than to use the correct translation, " Kneel before God in sacred vestments " ; to sing " The iron entered into his soul " rather than, " He was laid in irons ! " These are just examples of how the strictness of rationalism may be im-proved upon by the free spirit of mysticism. The same lifting of burdens is possible in the matter of listening to the reading of Lessons, some of which in their literal meaning are unedifying.

In answer to the complaint that much of the language used in the Church's worship is archaic, and some of it is exaggerated as an expression of feeling, it must be main-tained that to water down the expression of devotion to the level of the least devout is, to say the least, psychologically unsound ; for it is in the making of affirmations that habit and character are formed. In the expression of feeling, feeling grows ; and the nobler the expression the greater is the tendency engendered towards noble feeling. The up-lifting power of fellowship must also be taken into account. As everyone knows, we can experience emotions, as members of a worshipping body, which are beyond our unaided powers of devotion, but none the less genuine. It is not only that we may be helped by our friends and neighbours in the visible building where we pray ; we can be helped even more by the consciousness that while offering our imperfect adoration in the supreme Holy-Holy-Holy, we have the uplifting fellowship of the unseen hosts of " angels and archangels and all the company of heaven ". Secondly, the alternative to " archaic " language is up-to-date lan-guage ; which implies, in effect, a language which changes from decade to decade, if not from year to year. There is a mystic efficacy about language which is tried and tradi-tional, pregnant with devotion, as an old violin is pregnant with music ; and no glamour of modernity can take its place. If proof of this were required, it could be found in the fact that, with at most half-a-dozen exceptions, no really satisfactory collect has been produced in modern times.

The plea that grown-up people can infuse into the rather dull form of Morning Prayer a spirit of mystical interpreta-tion is no excuse for forcing that type of service on helpless children. What really matters at the present time is that children should not be deprived of their rights in worship by the selfishness and prejudices of their elders. Almost every criticism of Matins as an act of worship is wholly justifiable in the case of children. They cannot be expected to find methods of escape from the blood-thirstiness of some Psalms, the intolerable boresomeness of some Lessons, or the general dullness (as it seems to them) of a service without movement, colour, or dramatic symbolism. On the other hand, all these things, so dear and so profitable to children, are to be found in the Eucharist. It is simple, arresting, and romantic. Because it is mystical through and through in itself, and not merely by a mystical interpretation conferred upon it by the worshippers, it is emphatically the children's service.   To suggest that it is too holy for children is a false reverence : Jesus said, *Give not that which is holy unto the dogs ;* He did *not* say, " Give not that which is holy unto My children ".

Can these dry bones live ? Can an institutional form of religion, that had grown atrophied, be raised to life by the spirit of mysticism ?   The skeleton is there ; and there can be no body without a skeleton.   Institutionalism is essential, but it is not enough.   The questions to be faced in regard to public worship are not abstract or merely rhetorical. They are questions of life or death : *I have set before you life and death . . . therefore choose life . . . that thou mayest love the Lord thy God, and that thou mayest obey his voice, that thou mayest cleave unto him : for he is thy life and the length of thy days.*   The questions are being answered ; the choice is being made ; the beacon of Hope is alight.   More and more it is coming to be recognised that the Church is a worshipping community : that is the reason of its being.   Worship matters. In every parish this aspect of religion should be presented to and by God's people week by week, day by day.   That is the true witness of the parish church, the witness of worship.   All other activities, of philanthropy, of education, of social betterment, and every other good work are secondary.   Furthermore, they are dependent for their good on the due fulfilment of the premier duty.   Based on that conviction, a new spirit is animating the Church.   Once again, after a long interval of side-tracked energy, Christians are learning to put first things first.   The battle is joined.

In this struggle for true worship, the soldiers of the Cross owe a special debt to two men.   Percy Dearmer supplies the tactics, and Gabriel Hebert the strategy.   The titles of their best-known books are signs of the particular guidance that they have to offer.   In *The Parson's Handbook* Dearmer is concerned with tactics ; the ordering of the ministers and their equipment, the due place and function of the various units in the army of worship, the traditional drill which enables them to perform their separate functions without clashing, *decently and in order*; the co-operative carrying-out of a common and coherent purpose. Of course it is not the only handbook of tactics available for the would-be worshipper, but it is the pioneer of the present revival, and presents a scheme based loyally on the best tradition, but adequate to the fresh needs of our time. Hebert's *Liturgy and Society* is a greater book ; as the science of strategy is greater than the science of tactics. It takes a wider view, and looks more definitely to the ultimate goal. It is not surprising, therefore, to find it instinct with what may be called " The Higher Mysticism ", the spirit of first-hand religion *at work*, which is not content until all society is set on the ladder of holiness, and has its eyes opened not only to the angels ascending and descending to " succour and defend ", but also to the Beautific Vision which is the final goal of Christian worship. Any attempt to summarise this manual of spiritual strategy would be to do it injustice. The point to have in mind is that an upward movement in public worship has begun, and it is not without guidance : *Prophesy unto the wind, prophesy, son of man, and say to the wind, Thus saith the Lord God ; Come from the four winds, O breath, and breathe upon these slain that they may live. So I prophesied as he commanded me, and the breath came into them, and they lived, and stood upon their feet, an exceeding great army.*

No record of what mysticism is doing for the religious life of our time would be complete without some reference to Holy Silence. Silence is not a mere cessation of sound, a temporary lull, any more than peace is a mere cessation of war, an interval of preparation for fresh slaughter. Both silence and peace are positive, not negative. It would be a happier world if men could be brought to understand the great affirmative of peace. The religious life of mankind would be immeasurably strengthened by a right understanding and use of silence. It is an essential part of worship : nothing can take its place : and nothing has the right to oust it. Yet Christians, other than the Quakers, have long been defrauded of it. " The tyranny of the organist " is imposed on many congregations to such an extent that they have no moment for silent recollectedness from the beginning of the service to the end. It is an intolerable tyranny, which, however, will not be overcome until a larger number of worshippers have learned—and insist on being allowed— the *positive* blessing of silence.

It is a blessing which is quickly learned by experience. Times of united silence in which a few kindred souls meet together to wait upon God (preferably in His House), without even the formality of an opening or closing prayer, are enough to point the way. If every Christian is a potential mystic, he is also a potential appreciater of Holy Silence. The time is not far off when one part of the revival of the mystical element in public worship will be the opportunity given for silent prayer and meditation, passing into adoration. Worshippers will then discover that the atmosphere in which spiritual freedom is best found is the atmosphere of silence : *Be still then, and know that I am God.* Among all calls for improvement and enrichment in the spiritual life of the present generation, mysticism would claim priority for the use of silence, and institutionalism would offer no hindrance. Ordered vocal devotion is strengthened, and lifted to a higher plane by intervals of free silence.

There is a danger of being betrayed into trying to cover too wide a field in any survey of the relations between mysticism and institutionalism. There are so many fascinating by-paths to beguile the enquirer. There are so many trees to admire, that he fails to observe the significance of the wood. In this consideration of the subject which we have undertaken, we must not be betrayed in going outside our " terms of reference " to deal with individual devotion.

In order to avoid this danger of discursiveness, it is essential to keep in mind the great principles of religion, as laid down by von Hügel, to which reference is made in Chapter I. His contention that there must always be the three main "elements" in religious life is axiomatic. Starting from that, the supreme task of the Christian worshipper and worker is to see that the three elements are harmonious and co-operative ; for human nature is such that men seldom see the truth "whole", unless thay set themselves consciously and stedfastly to do it. It is a plain duty to try to make the proper adjustment of the three elements for ourselves and for others.

In the effort to do this, which is our present purpose, we may have been able to answer, for ourselves and for others, some of the questions with which we were confronted, and, in particular, the question of the joint-part that mysticism and institutionalism have to play in worship. The conclusion of the whole matter may be summed up : "What is the attitude of the mystic, as worshipper, to institutional religion ? " This is a difficult question, because the practice of the great mystics has differed widely in this matter. Perhaps we may say that the mystic, as such, is too strong a sacramentalist to need Sacraments, though he has no motive for rebelling against the institutional religion which shelters him, and in which he generally finds a real help and steadying influence. The true mystic goes about his daily work in the spirit of a worshipper. Every place is holy ground to him ; his work-table is an Altar, his common food a Eucharist. Human affections are allowed and intensified by being regarded as sacraments of the love of God, in which alone the soul realises itself. The common lot of suffering is sweetened and dignified by its association with the Divine self-sacrifice, the message of the Cross. It is thus impossible to separate his devotional life from his active life ; they flow into each other and are indissolubly connected.

None the less, the *writings* of the great mystics are mainly concerned with personal religion. They bear witness to mysticism in being rather than mysticism in doing. It is, however, the latter, derivative activity of mysticism that we have been chiefly considering in these pages. Only a true mystic can deal adequately with the former. But, that the more important side of the subject may not seem to be ignored, an appendix is permissible, and the two concluding chapters are essays, tentative and incomplete, in personal religion, or " what mysticism means to me " as a guide to understanding the Word of God.

CHAPTER VIII

THE HEAVENLY MANNA

" S PEECH ", declared the cynic, " was given us to enable us to conceal our thoughts." This saying has the characteristic smartness and falsity of cynicism. It is a prostituted platitude, the wrenching into superficial cleverness of one side of an obvious truth ; the platitude that words are an inadequate expression of our thoughts. There is a prejudice against platitudes, because they are dull ; perhaps it is more because the people who repeat them are dull. Anyhow the statement of obvious truths is a much less interesting exercise than the attempt to make the truths work. The application of platitudes to life is one of the most thrilling adventures that a man can undertake.

" Words are an inadequate expression of our thoughts " —this applies not only to the spoken word, but also to the written word. Even Christians who claim that the words of the Bible are inspired (however differently " inspiration " may be defined) do not pretend that they convey the fullness of the truth that they are meant to express. We need to use any faculties that can bring us into touch with the men behind the words, and the divine Inspirer behind the men. According to the old saying, we have got to read the Bible with the aid of the same Spirit whose aid enabled men to write it. Rationalism alone cannot reveal the full meaning of the written word of the Christian Scriptures.

Without attempting an exposition of what is meant by *Meditation*, or describing its technique, it may be said that the mystics, and indeed all devout readers of the Bible, have reached the conviction that understanding comes in proportion to the completeness of relationship between the reader and what he reads ; apprehension is not through the intellect alone. This is usually stated in the form that to make a fruitful meditation the reader must exercise, to the best of his ability, the faculties of imagination, intellect, and will : picture the scene, search for its meaning, respond to its appeal. If a man reads his Bible without any resultant activity of the will, he is in danger of doing himself more harm than good. *To him that knoweth to do good, and doeth it not, to him it is sin.*

Seeing then that every human faculty has to be brought into play if the fullness of God's message in Holy Scripture is to be understood, it follows that the interpretation revealed to one faculty alone will not have the monopoly of truth or of fruitfulness. " Textual Criticism " is a valuable line of study, but it will not by itself render a man *thoroughly furnished unto all good works.* On the other hand, imagination tinged with sentiment will not supply a complete understanding. Least of all can the will alone give us what we need ; for the reader who brings his will to bear on his reading, without imagination or intellect, will be imposing his prejudices on the Scriptures, and wresting them to his own purpose.

All this leads to the conclusion that the various approaches to understanding must be co-ordinated. It also, I think, forms a justification of some variety of interpretation. The same passage will not always convey the same message to every man. As there is both a rational and a mystical approach to the study of the Bible, so there may be both a literal and a mystical interpretation of it : and these are not contrary the one to the other ; they are co-operative aids to understanding and to response. As a wise Bible-student, one of the younger prophets of to-day, has said :

" Though we are accustomed to speak glibly of the reference of all temporal and natural life in the Middle Ages to the eternal and supernatural, we are not always so clear about the concrete result of that general framework of belief. In fact, as Huizinga shows, every action had its due place within a graded hierarchy of being.

Every material and physical occasion had its counterpart of meaning and of life in the supernatural life. One result of this was that the natural life was drenched in symbol. Nothing meant itself alone. In the interpretation of Scripture this complexity of meaning and value produced the magnificent fourfold structure of the literal, the allegoric, the anagogic and the spiritual. Modern ' scientific ' criticism laughs at the näivity and credulity implied in this four-pronged approach. It is quite certain that the detached methods of modern scientific research, whether in the realm of Scriptural interpretation or any other realm, would have been equally laughable, if not quite meaningless, to even the most tolerant and learned of mediæval scholars. I have still to be convinced that the barren fields of the modern scientific method can produce results for the human life comparable in richness of being—real richness, not the mere external addition of material comfort and convenience—to the other-worldly reference and the hierarchical splendour of the mediæval point of view." [15]

One of the most valuable contributions that mysticism has to make to religion in the present day is that of a revived revelation about the hidden and supernatural messages of the Bible. The excesses which made the " mystical " interpretation of Scripture synonymous with " fantastical " interpretation had brought the practice into disrepute. With due safeguards, it can be revived with great gain to the spiritual enlightenment of those who practise it in wisdom and humility. It has, as most Bible-students will agree, the sanction of our Lord himself. In order to give some indication of how anyone of ordinary gifts, and without any special mystical training, can turn this method of interpretation to good account, an attempt is here made to set down some of the thoughts suggested by a well-known story in the Old Testament (Exodus xvi).

Some three thousand six hundred years ago, a clan of Semitic people, in their migration from Egypt to Canaan,

fell on bad times. In the barren wilderness food ran short,
and they laid the blame on their leaders. One morning,
however, *when the dew that lay was gone up*, they discovered
on the ground *a small round thing*, white as coriander seed,
and with a taste like wafers made with honey. It was something they had never seen before. " Manna ", they exclaimed, which in English is, " What is it ? " That became
its name.

Human laziness is often glad to avoid the trouble of
remembering proper titles and names. " Manna " saves
definition ; hence its popularity as a term of reference.
" Have you seen old whats-his-name lately ? " is one way
of enquiring after a mutual friend, and quite a favourite
way. A housewife, meeting her crony coming out of the
butcher's shop, asks, " Have they any thingummy left ? "
—meaning, and being understood to mean, " offals ".
Fifty years ago, a man called Watts had a small tobacconist's
shop in an obscure street of Nottingham. Prospects were
poor : but one day he conceived the idea of having " Watts-
his-Name " inscribed on the signboard over his shop window.
Customers began to patronise Watts-his-Name's in increasing
numbers ; so that within a few years the one little shop
grew into a chain of big shops, all with the same compelling
name. Prosperity came to Watts. Other instances might
be given tending to prove that there is in human nature a
hankering after anonymity, a popularity of the pseudonym ;
or rather, a readiness to refer to persons and things in vague
terms without giving them a name.

This love of vagueness holds good in other ways : it is
easier to influence people by declaring that " they " say
(that it is unlucky to walk under a ladder) than by quoting
a definite decision on some matter made by specified in-
dividuals in the High Court of Justice. Human conduct is
swayed by public opinion in the form of " what will *they*
think of me ? " than by any other influence. In literature
a poem by " Anon." seems better able to pass muster than

one of equal merit by some third-rate writer whose name is given. Many grown-up men will remember that form of slang, popular in their schooldays, whereby everything was called by a name other than its true one.

To take a relevant instance, the word " mysticism " panders to this human weakness. It suggests something which concerns a mystery, or a secret, or even the vague lure of the occult. The fact that in Greek the word " mystery " came to mean a revealed secret does not over-throw the implication that the attraction of mysticism, for many people, lies in its presumed secrecy, its anonymity. To be so attracted is, of course, illogical ; for, after all, to hanker after a revealed secret is to be guilty of a kind of contradiction in terms : a secret revealed is no longer a secret.

The Israelites maintained the illusion of vagueness and secrecy about their God-given food, continuing to call it by a perpetual question, Manna—What is it ? It may have been partly a gesture of reverence, as well as a con-cession to the human weakness of which we have been giving examples. But there was, in truth, no uncertainty about what it was, whence it was, or how it was to be used. We cannot acquit ourselves of responsibility with regard to God's gifts by giving them non-committal labels. God's beneficiaries must find a definite answer to the question, What is it ?—not necessarily in word, but most necessarily in deed. God made clear the obedience He required in connection with His gift. He always does. Every Divine gift is a call to obedience ; because it expects a response. Every talent is given for use.

What is the eternal signification of this incident of the manna ? Can a mystical interpretation of it find its justi-fication in illumination shed on the path of Christian endeavour to-day ? Each reader of the story can only answer these questions for himself ; but we can help one another by pooling the experience of our meditations. We contemplate the same record, even though our interpretation of it varies as our temperaments vary.

First, then, the manna was *from God : Then said the Lord unto Moses, Behold, I will rain bread from heaven for you.* God is the all-Giver, and all that man receives is from Him. So there can be no harmony in life, no understanding of what life means, unless we cultivate the grace of receptivity. This is true with regard to all human needs, and their fulfilment. The harvest of the fields, whereby the body is nourished and sustained, is not due to man's foresight and labour alone. Man sows the seed ; God gives the corn. So it is with the harvest of souls : *Who then is Paul, and who is Apollos, but ministers by whom ye believed, even as God gave to every man ? I have planted, Apollos watered ; but God gave the increase. . . . For we are labourers together with God ; ye are God's husbandry* (or " tillage "). The acceptance of this principle means that the twin dangers of a sense of frustration in dearth, and an arrogant self-congratulation in plenty, are merged into a humble thanksgiving, and consequent equanimity of content and confidence. Thankfulness is the one unfailing source of happiness.

Secondly, the manna was for all alike ; not for the privileged few, not only for the deserving ; for God *maketh his sun to rise on the evil and on the good, and sendeth rain on the just and on the unjust.* Here, indeed, is an inexplicable mystery of Divine bounty which every sinner can interpret to his own comfort. Not only, however, to his own comfort : he is also obliged by the Christian law of reciprocity to share with others the riches which he has neither won nor deserved. *Freely ye have received, freely give.* There were no rich or poor among the manna-fed Israelites, no " haves " or " have-nots " ; but an automatic communism ; they gathered *some more, some less . . . and he that gathered much had nothing over, and he that gathered little had no lack.* Each found that he had got not more or less according to his gathering, but the exact amount according to his need.

There was an inevitability about the sharing which pre-
cluded either greed or envy. One pictures the Israelites,
like Londoners in the Kent hop-fields, going out by families
to gather in the manna, rejoicing in the change from the
daily drudgery of their long trek, drawn closer together by
their fresh interest. The refreshment was mental as well
as physical ; just as it is in the case of the jaded slum-
dwellers from East and South London when they make the
yearly exodus to their hoppers' camps.

Thirdly, the manna was definitely a *daily* bread.: *Moses
said, Let no man leave of it till the morning. . . . But some of
them left of it till the morning, and it bred worms and stank.*
Hoarding is an evidence of distrust of God's providence,
as well as an attempt to take unfair advantage of one's
fellows. There was to be no reserve put by in case God
thought better of His generosity. As there was complete
dependence ; so there must be complete trust. That is one
lesson of the model prayer taught by the Lord Jesus, " Give
us day by day bread enough for the day ". The true
response to bounty is not presumption. Nor can there be
any worse blasphemy than to try to take unfair advantage
of God's goodness, or squander His gifts. He has compassion on the hungering multitude ; He feeds them without
stint ; but there must be no waste : *Gather up the fragments
that remain, that nothing be lost.* The soldier who says, " There
is abundance of food in the Army ; we don't have to pay
for it ; let us throw what we can't eat on the dump," is
no true patriot. Presumption is the enemy : the Christian
who humbugs himself and others by presuming on God's
goodness and liberality is false to his profession. It is not
reverence but irreverent presumption which leads a man to
say, " I may be doing wrong, but God is so loving ; I can't
believe He would condemn or punish anyone : anyhow, *it
will all come right* in the end ". In a word, the story of the
manna is not just a record of Divine lavishness, but a record
of Divine discipline. The Israelites were under discipline

in respect to God's bounty. The measure of their privilege was the measure of their responsibility. Those to whom God had in fullest measure revealed His graciousness must beware of treating it lightly : *You only have I known of all the families of the earth : therefore will I punish you for all your iniquities.*

The final test of the Israelites' loyalty and obedience was imposed in the command to gather nothing on the Sabbath. To men who had been on the verge of starvation the utter trustfulness required was frightening : *Six days ye shall gather it ; but on the seventh day, which is the Sabbath, in it there shall be none.* It was a searching test, because every man of good-will responds more readily to a call to work than to a call to rest ; or rather, he is more attracted by an activity which is popularly recognised as work than by a hidden work which wins the praise of God more than the praise of men. In the interior life, the conflict is between self-seeking and self-sacrifice : *What shall it profit a man, if he shall gain the whole world, and lose his own soul ?* Externally, it assumes familiar, homely forms : in war time how many parish priests long to be in khaki ! Their whole desire is set on ministering, as chaplains, to the men of the Services, sharing their hardships and dangers, sharing the romance. Yet their loyalty and obedience have to stand the test of a command to remain at their conventional jobs ; trying to do what they have been doing for years—carrying on—but short-handed through their best workers being " on national service ", ministering to people whose nerves are on edge with anxiety and overstrain, faced with tired and sadly depleted congregations.

Or again, how difficult it is for an active woman to believe that patient continuance in the well-doing of prayer on the Lord's Day is a higher vocation than serving out dough-nuts and tea in the canteen ! Once more, how disappointed is the boy who finds himself, by bad luck in the ballot, relegated to the darkness, danger, and dirt of

a coal pit, when he would fain be in uniform, and among
pals of his own type !   He is not easily convinced that this
hidden work, to which he is called, is the work that his
country needs from him, and that his finest service for his
country is the sacrifice of self-will in unresentful obedience.
It is in such every-day affairs of like and dislike, of cheerful-
ness or complaint, that the test comes home.   Men need a
standard of values that will enable them to rise above the
shallow pragmatism of popular opinion.   Mysticism, as has
been already pointed out, supplies that standard, for it
refers all values to God.   It helps us to remember that He
has little use for our fussiness.   More often than we are
ready to believe His call is to that *quietness and confidence*
which is our true strength ;   because to obey that call is to
let God do His own work in His own way.

The particular mystical interpretation of this passage of
Scripture about the manna in the wilderness is not far to
seek.   It is given us by our Lord himself, as recorded in the
sixth chapter of the Gospel according to S. John :   *I am that
bread of life.   Your fathers did eat manna in the wilderness, and
are dead. . . . I am the living bread which came down from heaven.
. . . Except ye eat the flesh of the son of man and drink his blood, ye
have no life in you.*   Mystical the words of Christ may be ;
but they are not illusory, vague, or unpractical.   God's
bounty has a defined channel, as the previously bewildered
disciples learned at the Last Supper.   The gift of eternal
life, to be shared with their Master, did not depend on their
ability to understand all His teaching.   Doctrine was not
the Bread of Life.   Nor was righteousness.   It was, and is,
a free gift mediated through an *effectual* sign of grace ;   that
is to say, a sign which effects what it signifies.

Of this the teaching of the Church of England, in
Article XXV, is most admirably clear.   The Food is food ;
and, as food, nourishes.   Just as truly as the bodies of the
Israelites were sustained by the manna, so the souls of
Christians are sustained by the Body and Blood of Christ

which are " verily and indeed taken and received by the
faithful in the Lord's Supper ". It is a Food about which
there is no question, or should be no question. " What is
it ? " is not the response that loyalty would make to the
Master's promise. His words must be either accepted or
rejected ; they cannot be explained away. If they are
accepted in simple faith, wonderingly, then all the details
of the simile He uses fall into place, like the pieces of a puzzle.
What was revealed in the incident of the manna has its
significance for the Christian communicant.

The application is not difficult, for experience proves
that mysticism always has a practical side : but it requires
that mystical spirit of enlightenment which can see the
eternal in the temporal. The whole matter can be simply
stated : (1) One definite historical revelation of God's love
finds its antitype in another, and its fulfilment ; (2) Each
disciple of Christ can trace the fulfilment in detail, according
to his own needs and his particular illumination ; (3) All
that need be undertaken here, is to point out, in general
terms, the lessons that the Old Testament has to teach in
our interpretation of the New Testament.

The manna was from God : the Food in the holy sacrament is from God ; and therefore Divine. It is not made
Divine by human faith, but by God's power. Whatever
Jesus made the bread and the wine at the Last Supper,
He makes them at every celebration of the Holy Communion.
" The unworthiness of the priest hindereth not the efficacy
of the Sacrament " : neither does the unworthiness (or
ignorance) of the communicant banish from the Sacrament
its reality. If it did, as some pretend, S. Paul would have
been guilty of a grievous error in warning his readers that
*he that eateth and drinketh unworthily, eateth and drinketh damnation
to himself, not discerning the Lord's body.* There is no " damnation " (judgment) involved in eating and drinking
ordinary bread and wine.

Secondly, the Sacrament is for all, as the manna was.

Therefore, it is a misuse of the heavenly food to confine it to a few select folk. It is not, as many Protestants seem to think, a reward for being good ; but, as the Church teaches, a help to being better. Food is for the hungry, the heavenly manna for sinners who need it most, rather than for those who can enjoy the flesh-pots of Egypt : " Ye that do truly and earnestly repent you of your sins . . . draw near ". The Church takes her Master at His word : *Come unto me, all ye that labour and are heavy laden. . . . I will give you rest : I came not to call the righteous, but sinners.* The Bread of Life is for all who feel their need.

Once again, not only is it meant for all, but it is accessible to all. Every Israelite had his portion of the manna. Every Christian may, if he sincerely wills it, have his portion of the Bread of Life. Furthermore, because every child of God is a potential mystic, the way is open for all to learn not only the blessedness but also something of the meaning of God's greatest Gift. The child of God does not have to pass through long probation and testing discipline, like the initiates of the Greek or Egyptian mystery cults. God moves to man, not man to God. So the gifts of God are free ; and the thought that they are " too good to be true " is dishonouring the Giver. That the manna was God's free gift for their sustenance was enough for the Israelites to know. Its value was proved in its use. It did sustain them, and so turned their thoughts in thankfulness to the Sustainer. It was just one manifestation of the force of love which sustains the universe in all its parts. Looked at as an element in the Divine purpose, the manna was not abnormal, just as mystical insight is not abnormal, and sacramental grace is not abnormal, and " miracles " are not abnormal. The relation of the part to the whole, of " signs " to their signification, of the outward and visible sign to the inward and spiritual grace, of the channels of grace to their Source—all these manifestations of a perfect will are harmonious, natural consequences of the superna*ural. Mysticism never encourages surprise at God's gifts, but only awe and love for the Giver.

The meaning of God's gifts is unfolded in their use. It is only by " tasting and seeing " that we discover *how gracious the Lord is ;* as the Israelites found out in the wilderness. For them, the proof of the manna was in the eating—and the answer to their question, " What is it ? " It is in inability to make the venture of faith, to taste and see, that many aspirants go astray, and tread the path of disappointment leading to the abyss of despair. They confuse acceptance with use, and expect to know joy and peace in the Sacraments, or in the mystical approach to God, without troubling to prove them by use. They would like to lay in a store of heavenly manna, and avoid all further trouble. But, from the first, that was forbidden. The whole conception of any selfish enjoyment of the Divine bounty, or of bargaining with God even in its most disguised forms, is a wrong conception. *What hast thou that thou didst not receive ?* asks S. Paul. He goes on to show that what we have received must be related to Him from whom we have received it by a growing spirit of service, daily *use* of daily bread. It is in the daily gathering of the manna, the regular and sustained response to grace, that the life of the soul is invigorated into its true destiny. The work that each has to do is given him, with power to do it. The test of each man's response is not the greatness but the thoroughness of his work. The mystical expression of this principle is given, with memorable force, by William Blake :

> " He who would do good to another, must do it in minute particulars. General good is the plea of the scoundrel, hypocrite, and flatterer. For art and science cannot exist but in minutely organised particulars, and not in generalising demonstrations of the rational power. The infinite alone resides in definite and determinate identity."

The persistent doing of little things well is the essence of Christian perseverance, and the path of life for most Christians.

It is, then, in the will that the guidance of the Spirit is fulfilled. *He will guide you into all truth—Ye shall know the truth, and the truth shall make you free :* free, not for sloth or enjoyment, but for service. Illumination must crystalise into purpose : duty does not shine in the Milky Way, but lies in the path at our feet. That is where the disciples of Jesus can find it : *I pray not that thou shouldest take them out of the world ; but that thou shouldest keep them from the evil.* Mysticism does not aim at withdrawal from the world, but at withdrawal from the evil of the world. It does not postulate a special and a different world : it takes the world as it finds it (as Jesus did, and Socrates dared not) and strives to transform it into the Kingdom of God. Illumination without purpose is as futile as purpose without illumination. Nor must it be forgotten that, in meditation on the Scriptures there is more wisdom, *and more will-power*, in the simple faith of mysticism than in the complex doubt of rationalism : *The secret things belong unto the Lord our God : but those things which are revealed belong unto us and to our children for ever, that we may do all the words of this law.*

CHAPTER IX

"IT IS GOOD FOR US TO BE HERE"

IT is a pleasing concept to imagine that by inserting the Feast of the Transfiguration into the 1928 Prayer Book institutional religion, as represented by the Church of England, paid a trifle of the debt that it owes to mystical religion. What seemed like an act of restoration was half-consciously an act of reparation. The Christian calendar was incomplete without some commemoration of an event which has always meant so much in the religion of experience. It is no wonder that the Transfiguration has ever made a special appeal to mystics ; for both its setting and its implications are in accord with their manifestation of the approach to God. They do not need to enquire whether it was vision, or illusion, or hallucination, or projection from the sub-conscious. Their own spiritual experience has taught them, somehow, that the event described in the Gospels must be true. Even those Christians for whom the word " mysticism " has little meaning would, none the less, re-echo Peter's words, *It is good for us to be here*, as they contemplate the event. Though they know not what to say, and their understanding is dim, they are conscious that for them, and for all, the Vision on the Mount has some beneficent lesson.

The English version of Peter's cry is inadequate to express the full meaning of the Greek word (καλόν) translated " good ". He did not mean only that it was good for them to be there in the sense of its being advantageous ; as we say to a convalescent that it is good for him to take a tonic, or that it is good for an over-worked doctor to take a holiday, or that discipline is good for a mischievous child. The root-meaning of the word is " beautiful " : and as harmony of sound is the essence of beauty in music, and harmony of colour and design the essence of beauty in art, so harmony with the will of God is beauty in conduct, or goodness.   It spells seemliness of life.   This cry, therefore, must be interpreted according to the full breadth of the word.   Peter felt that he was sharing in " the beautiful " (τό καλόν), that he was being given a taste of the perfect harmony of the Divine life.   The veil of mystery, which enveloped the incarnate Lord, was for the moment lifted, and His friends were given a sight of that reality of beauty, goodness, truth, and power, which is the consummation of the mystic's quest.   Their vision was, is, and will be, a present reality for those who have eyes to see.

The eternal present of the things concerning the Son of Man, *the Lamb slain from the foundation of the world*, is a conception woven into the very fabric of the religion of experience. Peter was but groping after this conception.   He was far from having reached the stage of full illumination.   The impetuosity of his words, as on other occasions, outstripped his conscious convictions.   The cry of faith was counterbalanced by the cry of fear, *Let us make three tabernacles.*   He feared that the present might vanish into the past.   The conception of eternity, the ever-present, was not yet revealed to his spirit.   His desire for three tabernacles was a reversion to that inadequacy of faith, that Jewish prejudice, which wanted to keep not only Jesus, but also His two witnesses from the past, Moses and Elijah, and to put them all on the same level.   Once again the impetuosity of his words had got ahead of coherent thought ;   his fear betrayed his faith.   But we may be sure that the faith was there.   Dr. Latham's words are true of all three of the privileged disciples :

" Their Master's spiritual exaltation did not put a gulf between Him and them ;   because they were so far one with Him that they were in a measure uplifted together ;   what was His was also in part their own ;   whether in earth or heaven, or wherever their Master's kingdom should be, they felt sure they must be by His side. They could not be estranged from Him by awe of a newly discovered dignity, for they had been sure of His possessing this before, and only wondered that it had not come more patently to light." [16]

Nevertheless, their reaction to the vision was a trembling one. Even their spokesman wist not what to say ; for they were sore afraid.

The alternating pulse of faith and fear in face of holy things is a persistent part of our human make-up. Faith falters in believing its own beliefs, and distrusts itself—" I falter where I firmly trod ". So nothing is more natural than the desire, shared by so many, to localise and perpetuate the presence of the Master by some human device. But the vision on the mount could not be caged in three booths. The Son of God can never become " the prisoner of the tabernacle ". It is true that, to meet our human weakness, He may and does grant a real presence in His covenanted way. It is at our peril, however, that we interpret His promise in a monopolist fashion, making real absence the alternative to real presence. " Presence " is a word which cannot be transferred from the human to the Divine order without some serious effort to understand that presence in the realm of time and space is vastly different from the presence of spirit in eternity and infinity. For us, the wisest and humblest definition of our faith in God's presence is that " Spirit is, where Spirit works ".

Words fail us when we try to describe the Mystic Way or the Divine Presence. They seem to be almost a mockery of our effort. To write of such things savours of presumption. But when literature fails, it sometimes happens that music or art achieves something more in the way of success. What music can do only the musical know. Art makes a wider appeal ; and in the work of a mystical painter it has given us an interpretation of the Transfiguration, which

goes beyond the power of words. Those who have visited
the friary of S. Marco, in Florence, will remember Fra
Angelico's wonderful fresco of the Transfiguration. In the
centre is the shining figure of Christ ; a little below, the
dim, majestic forms of Moses and Elijah ; in the foreground
kneel the three apostles in adoring fear ; while on either
side stand the Blessed Virgin and S. Dominic. With true
spiritual insight the saint, who knelt to do his painting, has
portrayed the Vision as revealed to the past, the present,
and the future. For the vision of God is, in its very nature,
eternal :

The glorious company of the Apostles praise Thee ;
The goodly fellowship of the Prophets praise Thee ;
The white-robed army of Martyrs praise Thee ;
The holy Church throughout all the world doth acknow-
    ledge Thee, the Father of an infinite majesty.

What was this great sight and what was its setting ? A
tradition, accepted by the earlier mystics, places the scene
of the Transfiguration on Mount Tabor. Later scholarship
gives, I think, a wider and more fruitful setting for the
incident. It has been shown that it is more probable that
it took place on one of the spurs of Mount Hermon. Jesus,
as the gospels record, had been in northern Galilee in the
neighbourhood of Bethsaida, and coming down from the
unnamed mount on which the Transfiguration took place
he found His disciples near Caesarea Philippi, which is
almost at the foot of Hermon. Tabor does not fit the
picture so well. It is in southern Galilee, an isolated hill of
no great height, " a low rounded knoll " which scarcely
fulfils the description of the place as a " high mountain ".
Nor would it provide, as securely as Hermon, the privacy
that Jesus sought. Whatever tradition may have to say,
the Bible account seems to justify the verdict of modern
scholars.

We can, therefore, picture the Carpenter and His three

fisherman friends ascending a ridge of the lofty snow-capped Hermon, in the cool of an August evening. They were weary after a day of toil and excitement, glad to be apart from the multitude, and to lift up their eyes to the hills from whence cometh the help of peace, and stedfastness, and purification. Looking back, as the sun set over the western sea, they would have on their right-hand the loved and familiar countryside of Galilee, and the villages which were home to them. To the left lay the harsher landscape of Iturea and Decapolis with its alien Hellenic cities, artificial and corrupt. Between the two landscapes, in the distant south lay that most beautiful of inland waters, the Sea of Galilee, the scene of their toil and of Jesus' early ministry. How much of all this outlook lay within their view that summer evening we cannot tell. One dominating picture, however, was certain ; ahead of them was the mystery of the mountain, the inspiration of Excelsior higher and higher up to the clouds.

The summit was never reached ; just as the summit of the Mount of Holiness is never reached in this life. It was at a halting-place that the vision came to them. So, too, was it a halting-place in the ministry of Jesus, a halting-place that was also a turning point. It marked a clear division between the ministry of service and the ministry of suffering. In Galilee He had been among His own folk, serving them. Slow though many of them were in response, and prone to misunderstanding, yet on the whole they were friendly folk ; *the common people heard Him gladly.* But after the Transfiguration, as He warned those who were present, He was to *stedfastly set His face to go to Jerusalem,* there to face suffering and the open enmity of those who in the end brought about His crucifixion. There was to be no smooth ascent from glory to glory ; but a descent into Hell in life and in death, before the final Ascension. Even after the night of vision on Hermon the four comrades were to descend, next morning, to a scene of sorrow and frustration.

Always the Mount of Calvary lies between the Mount of Transfiguration and the Mount of the Ascension.

To the mystic this is all familiar ground. He has traversed it himself. To him it is simply the emergence in history of his own experience. It might be called the sacrament of truth ; for it is the outward and visible sign of an inward and spiritual grace, the grace of the mystic ascent. The Scale of Perfection is set on Hermon. Every detail fits in, like the stones of a mosaic, to make the complete picture. First comes the steep ascent of the purgative stage, escape from creaturely ties and the claims of worldly life ; then, the halting-place, unexpected perhaps but chosen by the Master. Next comes the illuminative stage, the shining effulgence in which God is revealed as God. In this stage the cloud, which overshadowed them, has its place in the symbolism of the event. As the unknown author of *The Cloud of Unknowing* writes : " The higher part of contemplation (as it may be had here) hangeth all wholly in this darkness and in this *cloud of unknowing*, with a loving stirring and a blind beholding into the naked being of God himself only ". Furthermore, it is true to the nature of spiritual experience, as the mystics have always asserted, that the unitive stage in the ascent to God cannot and must not be dependent on ecstasy or even on vision. It was when the Transfiguration was over that *Jesus came and touched them . . . and when they lifted up their eyes, they saw no man, save Jesus only*. What more could they want ? He was all in all. They were alone with the One. The inward and spiritual grace sealed the outward and visible event. For them was fulfilled such a prayer as that of Christina Rossetti :

> As rivers seek a sea they cannot fill
> But are themselves filled full in its embrace,
> Absorbed, at rest, each river and each rill ;
>   Grant us such grace.

Here we have a reminder of that elementary truth, too often forgotten, that all trustworthy spiritual experience must be deep-rooted in prayer. Even if it were no more than a discipline of the soul, prayer would be essential ; but it is much more than discipline, it is inspiration.

True visions owe their worth to man's response to grace, in persevering prayer ; even when the perseverance is no more than a grim determination to keep in touch and tune with the Infinite, at all costs and under all discouragement. Prayer was, so to speak, the *sine qua non* of the Transfiguration : *Jesus took Peter and John and James, and went up into a mountain to pray. And as He prayed the fashion of His countenance was altered.* The new fashion of His countenance was revealed to those who prayed with Him. So it ever is. To all those who pray, and pray earnestly, there may come the illumination of a fresh and further vision of Christ, and a corresponding expansion of their own life in the Spirit : *We all, with open face, beholding as in a glass the glory of the Lord, are changed into the same image from glory to glory, even as by the Spirit of the Lord.* But there is no compulsion about the change. Like every part of God's will for our good, its fulfilment depends on our co-operation—the simple, loyal, constant obedience to the command to pray—will answering will. Thus, and thus only—and thus inevitably—the superhuman grows out of the human. Thus, man ascends the mount of his Divine destiny, in fellowship with the Son of Man. This ruling of providence upon which illumination depends—the kindling of the Divine spark, *already there*—is summed up by B. F. Westcott in a characteristically wise and pregnant comment : " The Transfiguration is the revelation of the potential spirituality of the earthly life in its highest outward form. . . . Here, as elsewhere, the Son of Man gives the measure of the capacity of humanity, and shows that to which He leads those who are united with Him."

What of those *two anointed ones*, prefigured on the screen of time by the prophet Zechariah, *that stand by the Lord of the whole earth ?* Their appearance implies that even on the

Mount of Vision there is the remembrance of an institutional side of religion. The Transfiguration is, in some ways, the most compelling focus of mystical symbolism. But, however mystical in its interpretation, it was an event which did not part company with the other sides of religion. The greater mystics never failed to insist that a due balance should be maintained, that the " three-fold cord " should not be broken. Richard of S. Victor voices the conviction of them all when he declares, " Even if you think that you have been taken up into that high mountain apart, even if you think that you see Christ transfigured, do not be too ready to believe anything you see in Him or hear from Him, unless Moses and Elias run to meet Him. I hold all truth in suspicion which the authority of the Scriptures does not confirm, nor do I receive Christ in His clarification unless Moses and Elias are talking with Him." The religion of experience can only be verified by the religion of authority.

It is not unreasonable to feel that the presence of these two witnesses must have exercised a stabilising influence on the minds of the three disciples. It brought the vision into a clearer perspective, and related it to the religious system in which they and their Master had been brought up. The two witnesses were, also, representatives—representatives of the Jewish Church, that highly developed, precisely ordered *institution. There appeared unto them Elijah with Moses, and they were talking with Jesus :* the event of the Transfiguration, timeless in its significance, was none the less rooted in the past. In the Divine order it developed out of the Jewish Church and its tradition. God's dealings with His chosen people had been embodied in the Law and in Prophecy. Moses represented the one, and Elijah the other. Both were institutional. The Law impinged on life at every point ; it was a systematised discipline covering the whole of human activity for the Jewish race. The moral maxims of the Decalogue were but one side of its claim, for it included the highly elaborate rubrical framework of ceremonial, as well as an intricate code of sanitary regulations. So that Moses has rightly been called " the father of sanitary science ".

Nor must it be assumed that the prophets were outside the institutional fabric of the Jewish Church. They were not just missionaries, who delivered an individualistic message in a state of irresponsible ecstasy. Still less were they self-hypnotised dervishes. On the contrary, they were, for the most part, members of a religious Order, recognised as men under discipline. Exceptions, like Amos, serve to prove the rule : *Then answered Amos, and said to Amaziah, I was no prophet, neither was I a prophet's son ; but I was an herdman, and a gatherer of sycamore fruit : and the Lord took me as I followed the flock, and the Lord said unto me, Go, prophesy unto my people Israel.* The fact that he found it necessary to justify himself for not being a prophet either by training or heredity shows how generally it was recognised that the prophetic ministry must normally be exercised within the confines of institutionalism, however elastic that institutionalism might be.

At first, in the history of the Jewish Church, the priests were not only the ministers of worship, they were also entrusted with the work of *teaching the children of Israel all the statutes which the Lord hath spoken unto them by the hand of Moses.* It was only when the priesthood failed in its duty of proclaiming the Divine righteousness that the Prophetical Order emerged. Samuel, himself a Levite, and almost certainly a priest, was the reformer who gave to the prophets a position of importance and responsibility which they had never before held. But the innovation was a work of reform, not of revolution. The prophets fell within the framework of the existing institution ; they were, by virtue of their office, ecclesiastics. For Samuel had taken measures to make his reforms permanent ; they were not meant merely to be effective to meet special needs, though in fact that is the side of their activity which is most prominent in

the scripture record. As a wise founder, Samuel had
instituted Companies or Colleges of prophets : and the
prophets, having been themselves trained and taught,
were given the task of teaching others.

I am not, here, making an attempt to give a full and
balanced account of the prophetic office or order and its
history. All that I am trying to do is to cast doubt on the
popular assumption that the prophets were the enemies of
institutionalism ; or that Elijah, on the Mount, was less
representative of the Jewish Church than Moses was.
Under the Old Covenant, as under the New, *The spirits of
the prophets are subject unto the prophets. For God is not the
author of confusion, but of peace, as in all churches of the saints.*
It is wronging the prophets to imagine that they were
in any degree like wild dervishes. Their task was a task
not of destruction, but of construction ; they had their
contribution to make towards peace and orderliness within
the church of God—not least by their " cleansing of the
Temple ".

The vision of the transfigured Christ was compassed about
by witnesses, who had been leaders not only in mystical but
also in institutional religion. This helped the disciples to
understand something of the future responsibility which their
sharing of the vision would lay upon them, the responsibility
of fitting the vision into the pattern of daily life. As the
climax of mystical religion is that a man is raised out of
himself into adoration, so, on the other hand, the aim of
institutional religion is the perfecting of a man's life, as he
is in himself and among his fellows. It follows, therefore,
that if the two sides of religion are duly recognised, the
Mount of Vision will always prove the Mount of Holiness.
The two (or three) loyalties of the religious life are not
parallel in their course : they are converging, for all alike
lead to God. It is important, therefore, before considering
the practical application of what the disciples learnt on the
Mount, to glance at the third of these converging loyalties ;

though it is not our immediate concern, and is outside our general plan.

Can anything relevant be said as to how the rational or intellectual element in religion is involved in this sacrament of Transfiguration ? The first point that calls for notice is that the event followed immediately after Peter's avowal of a creed ; and creeds are, for those who avow them, rational statements of fact as well as professions of belief. Peter's intellect had been at work on the problem of who Jesus really was ; and though the full enlightenment came, as Jesus said, from *My Father which is in Heaven,* nevertheless it was an enlightenment of the thought which was already at work. Revelation is God's reward for honest and fearless thought. A short time before the Transfiguration, Peter could do no less than proclaim the conviction he had reached, *Thou art the Christ, the Son of the living God.* But it was a creed which had not been reached by easy short-cuts ; and it required the noblest courage to proclaim it, a courage that fitted him for the confirmation of his faith by vision. In their ascent of the Mount the disciples were fortified by faith, a rational faith ready for the reward of its own establishment. They walked by faith, and they were rewarded by sight. The rational element in their religion was reinforced ; and many things which had been dim became clear.

They began to understand that Jesus was not so correctly God and Man as God in man. They were able to interpret the Transfiguration as the withdrawal of a veil rather than as the bestowal of a glory from outside. *His face did shine as the sun*—not as the moon which shines by reflected light, but as the sun which pours forth its own inherent light. They learned that much of their belief was above reason, though not contrary to reason ; and that it was reasonable to admit that things Divine cannot be fully apprehended by human minds. The inexplicable became rationalised. As regards the visible event, it may be said that just as after the Resurrection the spiritual body of Christ was temporarily materialised to establish faith ; so at the Transfiguration, the material body was temporarily spiritualised to establish faith. The change was, as it were, anticipatory. But the spiritual essence is always there ; and the change can be rationally understood.

This is, I think, one explanation of the Father's proclamation, *This is my beloved Son : hear Him.* It was a reminder that the inspiration and guidance of their life were to be found not only in the institutional authority of their accredited teachers, not only in the light of the mystic vision, but also in the voice of Truth itself. But always it must be borne in mind that in these matters there is no weighing up of rival claims. In the approach to God no one road is sufficient. It is balance rather than precedence that is to be sought for, in planning our use of the ways, and in responding to *the manifold grace of God.* The three elements in religion make their appeal to men of different temperaments with varying force. This we know from introspection, and from observation. We can see the danger of exaggeration, the foolishness of looking for a monopoly of value in any one of these elements by itself.

It is probable that the three disciples on the Mount were temperamentally institutionalists. They were loyal Jews, wedded to the traditions and practices of their past. Their outlook was fundamentalist. This exaggeration, we may believe, was rectified by the blinding vision of the present Lord. Two of the elements of true religion were reconciled for them. Before they descended from the Mount, the third element was proclaimed for the completion of their religious life and experience. They had seen and heard the two greatest teachers of their Church and Nation. What would they not have given to learn from them some authoritative solution of the puzzles and difficulties that confronted them ! They had seen the " metamorphosis " of Him whom they had chosen as their present infallible teacher ;

or by whom they had been chosen as learners. Still, something was lacking—the Father's sanction now given in
a voice out of the cloud. Their way was set, and their future
assured.

It is not right, nor indeed possible, to separate what
happened on the mountain-side from what happened at the
foot of the mountain, where a strange scene of bewilderment
and seeming disillusionment awaited them ; no continuation
of the glorious vision, but the tiresome importunity of a
stranger and his epileptic son. They had experienced the
privilege of the open vision. Now they had to learn that
privilege always implies duty. It carries with it a load of
responsibility. The mistake we are tempted to make is to
imagine that the duty must be commensurate with the
privilege ; that we should be called upon to do some great
thing, because we have received some great gift ; whereas
the duty that awaits us is often dull and irksome, something
which seems scarcely worth while. It is none the less the
test of our loyalty, a test chosen by God. The rebuke of
Naaman's servants comes home to many of us, *My father,
if the prophet had bid thee do some great thing, wouldest thou not
have done it ? how much rather then, when he saith to thee, wash
and be clean ?*

So it was with the chosen three ; they had been in the
presence of their national heroes, Moses and Elijah ; they
had seen the revealed godhead of their Master, *When they
were come down from the hill . . . a man . . . cried out, saying
Master . . . look upon my son . . . a spirit taketh him . . . and it
teareth him . . . and I besought thy disciples to cast him out ; and
they could not.* The bathos of it must have shaken their
exaltation. After the uplift of the night before, they might
well have expected some striking manifestation of supernatural power ; for all the Twelve were intimate friends and
followers of Him whom they three had seen transfigured.
The nine who were left below had been commissioned for
the healing work. But God's way was not in accordance

with their expectation : they suffered an unexpected disappointment. Instead of being shown great wonders—
though Jesus himself did indeed reward the stranger's faith
by healing his son—they were recalled to the simple habits
and duties of institutional religion : Jesus said, *This kind
goeth not out but by prayer and fasting.* [Many scholars question
whether these were the actual words of Jesus, though there
is better MS. authority for " by prayer " than for " by
fasting " ; but at any rate they embody what the writer or
transcribers of the Gospel believed to be the teaching of
Jesus ; so they are to that extent authoritative.] It is in
accordance with the Divine ordering of the world that
inspired men should be reminded that mystical inspiration
is a means to an end, and that there are other means,
additional, not alternative, to the same end.

Duty is the end : there is work to be done. In those
words, spoken by Jesus or attributed to Him, emphasis is
laid on two of the Three Notable Duties of the Christian
life—Prayer, Fasting, and Almsgiving—about which his
teaching in the Sermon on the Mount is undoubtedly
authentic. Many people would class these duties under the
head of institutional religion. Some might wish to go so
far as to relegate them to the inferior position of " observances " ; defying, in fact, the Master's teaching. All
three are duties, essential duties. All three come under
the heading of institutional religion *in part.* Nevertheless
nothing is more certain than that the mystical and the
rational elements of religion must have their share in all
three.

It is not only in the devotional side of institutional
religion that the mystical spirit may, and must work for
good. So in considering the " three notable duties ", the
Churchman's orders-of-the-day, it is right to hold fast to
that standard of values which is mysticism. Something
has already been said about prayer, the duty in which
mysticism has its most obvious part. Less obvious, but

particularly necessary to observe at the present time, is the application of a more spiritual standard of values to almsgiving. There is no more mystical saying in the Bible than our Lord's commendation of the poor widow, with her almsgiving of two mites : *Verily I say unto you that this poor widow hath cast more in, than all they which have cast into the treasury : for all they did cast in of their abundance ; but she of her want did cast in all that she had, even all her living.* It was the standard of her almsgiving, not the amount of her alms, which mattered—the testimony of costingness.

Institutionalism provides the treasury, the opportunity for giving ; it also settles the destination of the gifts. But mysticism, as ever, supplies the standard of values. It is, therefore, a tribute to the growing spirit of mysticism, and a hopeful sign in the life of the Church of England, that an attempt is being made to spiritualise finance, and implement the true principles of almsgiving, treating this "notable duty" as a matter for serious thought. For in its true nature it is not just an irksome necessity ; neither should it be the casual response to some passing, sentimental impulse, as it all too often appears to be. It is a sacrificial privilege, a "token" of self-giving. The various freewill offering schemes which have been inaugurated of late years, with their insistence on the three essential marks of right method in almsgiving—"systematically, individually, proportionately "—bear witness to the growth of a better understanding, even if, as yet, they have not succeeded in making almsgiving fully sacrificial.

There is no sphere of Christian conduct in which the assumption that mysticism pays more attention to sentiment than to duty is more clearly contradicted than in this instance of the spiritualising of finance. After the last war, materialism exploited sentimentality to such an extent that, in some cases, clergy and church councils, mayors and corporations erected, as "memorials" to those who had made the supreme sacrifice, objects for their own comfort and convenience. If such a prostitution of sentiment is to be avoided after the second world war, it can only be by allowing the mystical standard of values to prevail.

Thirdly, fasting has affinities with both prayer and almsgiving. To the mystic the three notable duties appear inseparable ; they merge into one another. It could not be otherwise ; for they are just three aspects of the response of love to Love : unless they are that, they have no meaning. Fasting aims at purifying and purging the whole man— body, mind, and spirit—for prayer. That it can do so is the unquestionable experience of those who have made the experiment perseveringly. None the less, it must be ruled by order as well as by zeal ; that is its safeguard.

Whatever excesses individual mystics may have been tempted to commit, in the region of false asceticism, have been in defiance of the wise regulations of institutional religion, with its defined and graduated variety of obser- vance. The greater the pressure generated in the boiler, the greater the need of a safety-valve. Institutionalism provides a safety-valve, and much more, for the violences of spiritual endeavour. For example, under the general head of " Fasting " institutionalism differentiates between *fasting* in the strict sense of refraining from eating, and *abstinence* which entails only abstention from certain kinds of food. There are varieties and degrees of fasting, arranged by authority to suit times, circumstances, and temperaments. Excesses of asceticism, for instance, are curbed by the Church's motherly wisdom in making fasting a duty for certain times and seasons, and regulating the method of observing them. *There are differences of administrations :* . . . *there are diversities of operations.* But we cannot doubt that they are inspired by the same Lord. The Church, therefore, because she knows the temperamental differences of her children—that some would fast at all times if there were no ordered calendar of fasts and feasts ; that others, and they the vast majority, would fast at no times if they could fast at all times—adds the direction of institutionalism to the impetus of mysticism. Thus is fulfilled the old adage :

The Bible bids us fast ; the Church says "now".

To loyal Christians the unmistakable voice of authority is always a welcome voice ; for they know, by humiliating experience, that human weakness, as well as undisciplined human strength, ever seeks to evade indeterminate laws. Such evasion is the road to ruin. It is of God's mercy that He says to His children, *This is the way, walk ye in it.*

One practical application of a wise and loving regulation is exhibited in the tradition and custom of fasting before Holy Communion. Those who practise it are not trying to lay upon their brethren a burden heavier than they can bear. All they do is to seize for themselves' an opportunity and a privilege : an opportunity, because in the circumstances of modern life it is difficult to observe the fast days without falling into the danger of being among those who *appear unto men to fast.* So that, for many Christians, the one fast that can be kept strictly, and without fear of ostentation, is this fast before Communion, which, for the mystic, is a reminder that God *satisfieth the empty soul : and filleth the hungry soul with goodness.* In pointing out that fasting, in the technical sense of the word, may not be possible (for some people at any rate) except in this particular observance, I must not be misunderstood to mean that " abstinence " is not possible. I suggest that abstinence may be kept unostentatious, and made much more disciplinary, by eating cheerfully things that we do not like, rather than in giving extra trouble by insisting on certain forms of food which can be officially classified as *maigre.*

Again, just as fasting proves so great an aid to prayer that its value as an end in itself is often overlooked, so it seems to be regarded often chiefly as a means to an end in its connection with almsgiving. Men think of it in the terms of reckoning how much more food they can provide for others by going without their accustomed amount of food themselves. We go without certain things in order that others may have them ; qualifying for the mystical word of divine gratitude, *I was an hungred, and ye gave Me meat*. That, in truth and reality, should be one of the underlying motives for fasting. It is part of the mystic's imitation of Christ ; and of his self-identification with the poor and the hungry. Jesus became poor in order that we might become rich, in true riches. The follower of Jesus accepts hunger in order that he may sympathise with the hungry, and succour them, and eventually lead them to know that *man does not live by bread alone*. None the less, the notable duty of fasting is not fully explained or exploited by regarding it as an adjunct to philanthropy. It is an end in itself ; as all sincere mystics know.

To sum up : there must be no mistake about the radical importance of the " three notable duties ", both from the side of mystical religion, and from the side of institutional religion. Nor must there be any failure to recognise that each of the three duties is, in itself, distinct from the other two. We have no right to say that to pray is to fast, or that to fast is to give alms. The fulfilment of one duty does not justify the neglect of the others : and no one of the duties can be neglected without hindering our fulfilment of the others. In spite of the help that fasting gives to prayer and almsgiving, it is not merely an auxiliary. It is in itself a sharing with Christ : and sharing with Christ is the aim and the consummation of all religious endeavour. On the other hand, though each duty is distinct from the other two, none can stand alone. The Three Notable Duties form a bond between us and God ; and *a three-fold cord is not quickly broken*.

More and more, as it seems to me, in the course of our enquiry into the relationship between the various elements in religion, and more particularly our enquiry into the connection between mysticism and institutionalism, we have

been led to see that, like two rivers flowing into the same
estuary, these two elements find their combined fulfilment
in their outlet. That is to say, that as we come to understand these two methods of approach to God, our understanding is based on the identity of their objective. God is
the centre of life's circle. Towards that centre, the vortex
of holiness, His children are drawn by centripetal grace.
But it is in little things that the advance is made. Not on
the mount, but on the plain lies our daily duty :

> . . . not yet to man is given
> To rest upon the height ;
> 'Tis but a passing glimpse of Heav'n ;
> We must descend and fight.

Nevertheless, by the grace of God, out of the little things
great things emerge. The great things, as the Apostle of
the Gentiles wrote in his letter to the Romans, are *glory and
honour and immortality, eternal life*. To whom does he declare
that God will give them ? His answer, well worth ponder-
ing, is that it is to them who seek for these things *by patient
continuance in well doing*. It is they who learn " the glory of
going on ". So it is that, in preaching the sanctification of
the inevitable, the final witness of Mysticism to-day, and
at all times, is,—Blessed be Drudgery.

BIBLIOGRAPHY

WITH NOTES, REFERENCES AND ACKNOWLEDGMENTS

It is a thankless task to draw up a Bibliography in 1945, when so many books are out-of-print and unobtainable. The following list does not pretend to be a summary of the principal books on mysticism. It merely gives the titles of some of the books which have helped me most in writing *Mysticism: Old and New*, together with a few notes as to their contents and value.

I. MEDIÆVAL MYSTICISM

WALTER HILTON. *The Scale of Perfection* (Art & Book Co., 1901), reprint of an edition by Serenus Cressy, first published in 1659 ; has as introduction an admirable essay (with a strong Roman bias) on The Spiritual Life of Mediæval England by J. B. Dalgairns. It includes a short *Treatise written to a Devout Man*, which may be accepted as being Hilton's work.

The Scale of Perfection—edited by Evelyn Underhill (John M. Watkins, 1923) may be called the standard edition. Evelyn Underhill's Introduction is particularly valuable.

Both these editions differ, in some respects, from the earliest edition, printed 450 years ago by Wynkyn de Worde ; as I found from consulting a copy in the Rylands Library, Manchester. My own feeling is that the study of English Mysticism should *begin* with Walter Hilton ; and that if the student cannot appreciate *The Scale of Perfection* he had better relinquish the study.

RICHARD ROLLE. *The Life and Lyrics of Richard Rolle*, by Frances M. M. Comper (J. M. Dent & Sons, 1928).

The Mending of Life, edited by Dundas Harford (H. R. Allenson, 1923).

The Form of Perfect Living, rendered into modern English by Geraldine E. Hodgson (Thomas Baker, 1910).

The Fire of Love and The Mending of Life, edited by Frances M. M. Comper, with an Introduction by Evelyn Underhill (Methuen & Co., 1914).

Minor Works, edited by Geraldine E. Hodgson (John M. Watkins, 1923).

There are a number of other editions of works reputed to be by Rolle. The best guide, at present available, to the study of his writings is to be found in Frances Comper's *Life and Lyrics of Richard Rolle.*

LADY JULIAN. *Revelations of Divine Love*—edited by Grace Warrack (Methuen & Co., 1901), the standard edition which will not easily be superseded. Grace Warrack's Introduction is an illuminating account not only of Lady Julian, but also of mediæval mysticism in general.

Comfortable Words for Christ's Lovers—edited by Dundas Harford (H. R. Allenson).

THE ANCREN RIWLE, modernised by James Morton, with an Introduction by Abbot Gasquet (Alexander Moring, 1905). This quaint handbook of practical mysticism should be compared with Hilton's *Treatise written to a Devout Man.*

THE CLOUD OF UNKNOWING—edited by Justin McCann, with a Commentary by Augustine Baker (Burns, Oates & Washbourne, 1924). "Depth masked with simplicity" is the characteristic of this anonymous work. Its simplicity may deceive readers as to its depth. It is one of the mystical writings which may be "read, marked and learned", without being "inwardly digested". Only a few of those who think that they understand it have really penetrated its secrets ; but they are a happy few.

THOMAS À KEMPIS. *The Imitation of Christ.* There are innumerable editions of the *Imitatio. Prayers and Meditations on the Life of Christ,* translated by W. Duthoit (Kegan Paul, Trench, Trübner & Co., 1904). I am not qualified to give a judgment as to the authenticity of this, or of several other of the preceding books ; particularly those attributed to Richard Rolle.

II. MYSTICISM IN LATER POETRY

To give a list of the English mystical poets from the seventeenth century onwards would be an endless task. Traherne, Herbert, Quarles, Crashaw, Vaughan, Blake, Wordsworth, Patmore, Christina Rossetti, Francis Thompson, and T. E. Brown are some of the names that demand notice. Many of the best poems will be found in Anthologies. There are, also, some editions with notes or introductions of special value, of which only one or two can be mentioned out of many equally good :—

THOMAS TRAHERNE. *Poems of Felicity*—edited by H. I. Bell (Clarendon Press, 1910). This is in addition to Dobell's standard edition of *The Poetical Works*, of which the third, 1932, edition is the most complete.

HENRY VAUGHAN. *Sacred Poems*—with Biological Sketch by H. F. Lyte (Bell & Daldy).

WILLIAM BLAKE. *Selected Poems*—with an Introduction by Basil de Selincourt (Oxford University Press).
Among anthologies, one of the most satisfying is *The Spirit of Man*, compiled by Robert Bridges (Longmans, Green & Co.). Though not exclusively a collection of mystical or devotional writings, it contains some of the cream of mystical poetry and prose.

III. MYSTICISM IN LATER PROSE

THOMAS TRAHERNE. *Centuries of Meditations*—edited by Bertram Dobell (P. J. and A. E. Dobell, first printed 1908). B. Dobell's Introduction, though an excellent literary appreciation of Traherne's work, is written by one who " frankly admitted his want of sympathy with Traherne's theological convictions ". None the less, his discovery of the " *Centuries* ", and his labour of love in publishing it put all students of mysticism under an obligation of gratitude to him almost too deep for expression.

WILLIAM LAW. *A Serious Call to a Devout and Holy Life*, with an Introduction by C. Bigg (Methuen & Co., 1899)—this is a handy edition of Law's best-known work ; there are many others.
Selected Mystical Writings, edited with Notes and Twenty-four Studies in the Mystical Theology of William Law and Jacob Boehme— by Stephen Hobhouse (The C. W. Daniel Co., 1938). It would be difficult to over-estimate the value of this delightful book. It shows a penetrating understanding of Law and of his mysticism. Not the least of its achievements is that it relegates *A Serious Call* to its true position as only one, and that perhaps not the greatest, of Law's books of illumination. Moreover, it selects the vital passages of his teaching without in any way

weakening them by lifting them out of the wordiness which modern readers find irksome in the writings of a more leisured age.

The Works of William Law. In nine volumes (printed for J. Richardson, 1762 ; privately reprinted for G. Moreton, 1892). This beautiful edition is essential for the study of Law's teaching.

ARTHUR CHANDLER. *Ara Coeli* (Methuen & Co., first published, 1908).
The Cult of the Passing Moment (Methuen & Co., first published 1914).

EVELYN UNDERHILL. *Mixed Pasture* (Methuen & Co., 1933).
Concerning the Inner Life (Methuen & Co., 1926). These are two of the most typical of Evelyn Underhill's books of essays in mysticism, which are to be distinguished from her essays on mysticism.

E. HERMAN. *The Finding of the Cross* (James Clarke & Co.). Seven mystical meditations on the Cross, so precious that some readers have felt that here we have a modern Lady Julian—a proof that mysticism is not dead, and can find expression in the twentieth century.

RONALD MAXWELL. *Still Point* (Nisbet & Co., 1944), an interesting autobiographical side-light on the value of modern mysticism—quoted in Chapter VIII.

IV. BOOKS ABOUT MYSTICISM

WILLIAM RALPH INGE. *Christian Mysticism*—Bampton Lectures, 1899 (Methuen & Co.). The revival of interest in mysticism, which has been one of the most noteworthy features of religious life in the early part of this century, is due primarily to Inge's Bampton Lectures. They give the starting-point for the whole study of the subject, and remain the best starting-point. Ever since he kindled the torch in 1899, Inge has kept adding to its light. Among his many subsequent writings on mysticism, two of the most useful are—
Studies of English Mystics—S. Margaret's Lectures, 1905 (John Murray).
Personal Idealism and Mysticism—Paddock Lectures, 1906 (Longmans, Green & Co.).

E. HERMAN. *The Meaning and Value of Mysticism* (James Clarke & Co., 1915)—a really great book which reveals mysticism *from the inside* to an extent which sets it in a class by itself. It fulfils its title.

RUFUS M. JONES. *Studies in Mystical Religion* (Macmillan & Co., 1909)—written with a particular sympathy towards sects like the Waldenses, the Anabaptists, the Seekers, and even the Ranters ; it deals with a side of the subject that is interesting as showing some strange flowerings of the mystical root.

EVELYN UNDERHILL. *Mysticism* (Methuen, many editions). *The Mystics of the Church* (James Clarke)—probably no one has done more to promote the understanding of mysticism, at the present time, than Evelyn Underhill has, by these and other well-known books.

HELEN C. WHITE. *The Metaphysical Poets* (The Macmillan Co., New York, 1936), a piece of thorough and inspired scholarship, which puts the authoress in the very front rank of writers about mysticism.

ARTHUR CHANDLER. *First-hand Religion* (Mowbray & Co., 1922)—practical and devotional.

PERCY H. OSMOND. *The Mystical Poets of the English Church* (S.P.C.K., 1919).

H. L. HUBBARD. *Self-training in Mysticism* (Christophers, first published, 1921)—gives the advice and guidance that a beginner needs to make mysticism a power and blessing in his life.

ACKNOWLEDGMENTS

I have tried, by reference and quotation, to express my gratitude to the many writers who have made mysticism one of the absorbing interests of life ; above all, to Friedrich von Hügel, as shown in Chapter I. This book owes its main value, as I know, to the opportunity it gives of calling attention to better books ; as I have done to the best of my ability. Among those who have helped me with information and advice, my chief acknowledgment must be to my well-tried friend, the Rev.

John G. Stobbart, who has, of his constant kindness, read the MS.; and by his encouragement and discrimination enabled me to improve it. For permission to quote I have to thank particularly Mrs. Battiscombe, Mr. Massingham, Messrs. Constable, Chatto & Windus, Heinemann, Blackwood, Dobell, Sidgwick & Jackson, Burns and Oates, Hodder & Stoughton, Faber & Faber, and Batsford. If there are others whose names I have inadvertently omitted, or whose courtesy I have taken for granted, I tender to them also my sincere gratitude.

REFERENCES

1. *Charlotte M. Yonge*, by Georgina Battiscombe, p. 17 (Constable & Co.).

2. *Rational Living*, by H. C. King, p. 31 (The Macmillan Co.).

3. *Grey Eminence*, by Aldous Huxley, pp. 77-78 (Chatto & Windus).

4. *South*, by Ernest Shackleton, p. 209 (Heinemann).

5. *450 Miles to Freedom*, by Johnston & Yearsley, pp. 291-293 (Blackwood & Sons).

6. *The Spiritual Exercises of S. Ignatius Loyola*, by W. H. Longridge, p. 29 (Robert Scott).

7. Quoted in *A Mediæval Mystic*, by Scully, pp. 62-63 (Thomas Baker).

8. *Centuries of Meditation*, pp. 19, 29, 63; and *Poetical Works*, p. 301, by Thomas Traherne (P. J. & A. E. Dobell).

9. *The Everlasting Mercy*, by John Masefield, pp. 41-42 (Sidgwick & Jackson).

10. *The Works of Francis Thompson*, Vol. II, p. 21 (Burns & Oates).

11. *The English Countryman*, by H. J. Massingham, pp. 113-114 (Batsford).

12. *The Word of God and the Word of Man*, by Karl Barth— translated by Douglas Horton, pp. 111-112 (Hodder & Stoughton).

13. *The Bishop's Confession*, by Hugh Shearman, p. 172 (Faber & Faber).

14. *Liturgy and Society*, by Gabriel Hebert, p. 7 (Faber & Faber).

15. *Still Point*, by Donald Maxwell, p. 47 (Nisbet).

16. *Pastor Pastorum*, by H. Latham, p. 344 (Deighton, Bell & Co.).

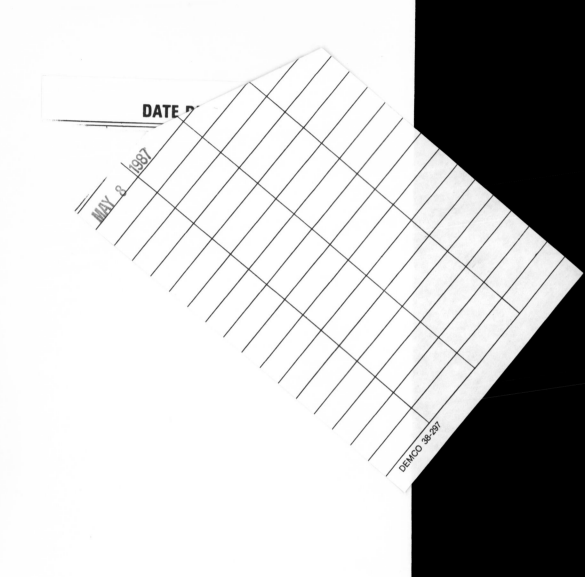